Field Guide to New England Barns and Farm Buildings

Field Guide to

New England

Barns

and

Farm Buildings

THOMAS DURANT VISSER

University Press of New England

HANOVER AND LONDON

University Press of New England, Hanover, NH 03755
© 1997 by University Press of New England
All rights reserved
Printed in Singapore
5 4 3 2 1
CIP data appear at the end of the book

CONTENTS

3 Outbuildings 105

4 Buildings for Feed Storage 123

5 Other Farm Buildings 141

PREFACE

The purpose of this field guide is to help residents, travelers, and scholars discover the rich rural heritage of New England before the surviving architectural evidence of this history is lost. As a scattered collection of artifacts, historic farm buildings can provide glimpses into the region's past. By providing clues for deciphering the many layers of history spread over the rural landscape and by showing how farm buildings fit into broad regional patterns, I hope to help observers see beyond a simple "then and now" nostalgic view of the past and instead realize the wonderful insights that can spring from an understanding of the evolution of our rural heritage.

While field guides to wildflowers use blossom color as the key to identify plant species, this field guide sorts vernacular farm buildings by their type, based on their form and use. Recognizing that these vernacular buildings are products of a diverse, complex, and fluid culture, this guide intentionally avoids using names that imply a direct ethnic or geographical lineage. (An exception is the commonly used "English barn" type name.) For this reason, the names of farm building types offered here tend principally to be descriptive of form and use.

The book is the product of the field research conducted in the six New England states—Maine, New Hampshire, Vermont, Massachusetts, Rhode Island, and Connecticut. To gather a representative sampling of the surviving physical evidence, the following methodology was developed. Within each state specific representative areas were selected for intensive study based on their association with past farming activities and the amount and integrity of the surviving architectural evidence of this history. For these intensive studies, "windshield" surveys were conducted along the highways and backroads of the areas. Both typical and distinctive examples of farm buildings and their characteristics were noted and photographed. The thousands of photographs obtained through this field research provide the primary source of comparative evidence and the bulk of the images for this work. Although the captions for some of these photographs provide the exact date of construction when known, many of the dates are approximations based on physical evidence and the general historic context, rather than on documented historical information. A margin of error of about ten years should be assumed when the term "circa" is used in these captions.

Major primary sources of published historical information about farming and farm buildings in New England include such agricultural newspapers as *New England Farmer, Maine Farmer,* and *American Agriculturalist.* These and other weekly and monthly periodicals provided agricultural news, practical information, and entertainment to nineteenth-century farm families. Their correspondence columns offer rich glimpses into the motivations and concerns of generations of New Englanders.

For those readers who may enjoy exploring old or abandoned barns, perhaps a few precautions are in order. Some deteriorated barns may be unsafe to enter. Hazards include weak floors (especially in areas covered with wet or rotten hay), rusty nails, pitchforks, burdocks, nettles, and farm dogs. Please respect the rights of the owners. Few of the buildings shown in this book are open to the public; however, most may be viewed from public roads.

With an awakening interest in New England's rural landscape and historic farm buildings, many recognize that these irreplaceable assets deserve greater protection and stewardship if this legacy is to be passed on to future generations. I hope this guide will help build a greater appreciation for this threatened resource.

Acknowledgements

Foremost acknowledgments are due to my father, William W. Visser, who provided the artwork, text editing, design guidance, and invaluable support throughout this project.

A partial list of those other persons who have made special efforts to assist with this project includes: Sheila Visser, Paul Bruhn, Eric Gilbertson, Michael Auer, Suzanna Zirblis, Curtis Johnson, Robert McCullough, Elsa Gilbertson, MaryJo Llewellynn, Nancy Boone, Jan Lewandowski, Kirk Mohney, Pamela Kennedy, Jack Shannahan, Mrs. Potter Noyse, Skip Sellow, Philip Gibbs, George and Diana Davis, Philip Dole, David Barber, William Bentley, Lisa Hartmann, Renee Viers Harrison, Erik Hanson, Jane Wil-liamson, Tyler Gearhart, Robert Sloma, Karen Peterson, Jack Watts, Reed Cherington, Russell Tilley, Clinton Reichard, Steven Barner, Mark Griffith, Tom Bassett, Polly Darnell, and John and Virginia Visser.

I would also like to acknowledge the support of the faculty and staff of the History Department, the College of Arts and Sciences, the Academic Computing Center, and the Bailey-Howe Library at the University of Vermont, as well as my students in the UVM Historic Preservation Program, and the owners of all the farm buildings shown in this book.

Funding for the research on this project was provided in part by the National Endowment for the Arts, Design Arts Program, a federal agency. Their support is gratefully acknowledged.

August 1996   T.D.V.

Fig. 1-1. Dairy farm with mid-nineteenth-century barns in Franklin County, Vermont.

The architectural legacy of New England's rich agricultural heritage awaits discovery across much of the region's landscape. Whether surrounded by hay fields or scattered through developed residential areas, historic barns and farm buildings linger as vulnerable survivors of the past. Yet before these buildings vanish, each has a story to tell. Together they provide a fascinating window into the cultural traditions and technological innovations that helped shape the history and landscape of New England.

Since written information about the history of specific farm structures is usually scarce, the best source of historical evidence is often the building itself. This chapter discusses some ways to estimate the age of a building through a careful examination of its construction materials, frame design, and architectural features. By correlating such bits of evidence with an understanding of the evolution of building technology and farming practices, it is often possible to piece together the history of a barn. Reading the history of a structure from physical evidence can be challenging. Often one must play the role of a detective to decipher clues of the past through observations of intermingled layers of evidence and alterations.

Usually, the design and types of materials used in a building indicate the age of construction, but New Englanders often used salvaged boards and old timbers when rebuilding their barns. Although unraveling this contradictory evidence can pose a challenge to researchers, a careful examination of the recycled materials may reveal the type and size of the building that was torn down. Thus, a large barn built in the late nineteenth century might have hand-hewn beams from a farm's original late-eighteenth-century barn.

3

Fig. 1-2. Circa 1790 English barn, Westford, Vermont. Around 1900 this barn was moved onto a new foundation, with cow stables in the basement. The original main door opening was located in the middle of the side wall between the posts behind the barrel.

Wear patterns on floor boards, empty mortises in timbers, and "ghost lines" on walls may reveal missing interior features. A bright flashlight and a camera with a flash are valuable tools for barn research. A careful walk around the farmstead may even reveal stones marking the footprint of the earlier barn.

From the outside the most effective identification procedure for vernacular farm buildings is to first determine their function, based on the size, shape, location, and distinctive exterior features. Examples of the major types of historic New England farm buildings are illustrated in this field guide.

Design Traditions, Fashions, and Innovations

Before exploring the evolution of farm building design in New England, perhaps we should ask: Who decides how a structure is designed and built? What factors influence these decisions?

Certainly, the answers are complex. The intended uses of the building, the siting options, the availability of materials, and the budget all influence design decisions by the owner. In addition, the farmer could be influenced by suggestions from family members and friends, designs completed by neighboring farmers, and perhaps recommendations offered in agricultural newspapers and other publications.

Although some New England farmers had the time, talent, tools, and experience to work professionally as carpenters or builders, for most farmers construction work was limited by their busy schedules. Winter often allowed time for logging and for hewing timbers, but only a few weeks in the early summer, between the planting season and the haying season, were available to launch major construction projects. For these, farm owners typically employed a contractor or master builder to oversee the project and design the timber frame and carpentry details.

Preparations for building a large barn could take years of saving and collecting materials. Some farmers harvested their own trees for the boards and timbers that were sawn or hewn to the dimensions specified by the master builder. After helping to plan the building with the owner, often months or years in advance, the master builder would arrive with a skilled framing crew. Within several weeks the timbers would be cut and the frame erected. Barn raisings were occasionally large social events, with scores of neighbors and friends available to lend a hand (see fig. 1-22). Most small farm buildings, however, were probably swiftly erected with the deliberate work of less than a half dozen workers. The owner would typically hire other tradesmen to prepare the foundation and do the finish carpentry. Farmhands and family members often helped with site work, raising the frame, laying floors, and boarding and shingling the building.[1]

The role and influence of skilled master builders, timber framers, and carpenters in the design of vernacular architecture is often ignored. The occupations typically required a period of training through a lengthy apprenticeship. As early as the seventeenth-century colonial English settlement of New England, these specialized tradesmen were among those actively recruited for voyages to the New World.[2]

By comparing the architectural features of farm buildings in old England and New England, we can see that early colonial farmers and their barn builders generally followed the traditional English building designs that were common to their original home regions, with innovations made for the harsher climate and availability of construction materials. Some features of early New England farm architecture can be traced back to the Elizabethan and medieval eras. An example is the basic design of the barn. Following a plan used from the Middle Ages for the storage and processing of grain harvests, the interior of the old English barn was typically divided into three sections with large storage bays on both gable ends. Separating the bays was a central wooden threshing floor aligned with pairs of hinged doors on the front and rear eaves sides. This design would allow farmers to bring wagons into the barn to unload the grain or hay and then drive forward to exit.

Fig. 1-3. As this 1830s architect's rendering of a picturesque "Old English Barn" suggests, barns built in Elizabethan England often featured gable-roofed "porches" to shelter the side entrances.

Early New England farmers modified the old English barn design by combining the functions of both the English grain barn and the cow stable into one larger building. Known simply as "the barn," the practicality of the design is reflected by its lack of change for nearly two centuries.

The so-called English barn design built in New England before the early nineteenth century balanced the functional and structural needs of the building with an aesthetic that echoes a medieval English heritage. Each piece of the barn frame was handcrafted for its specific location and function. Squat posts and oversize beams supporting thin, tapered rafters and purlins express a hierarchy of proportion. Smooth surfaces of adzed timbers contrast with the raw, natural textures of unfinished log floor joists.

Rather than introducing overtly stylish embellishments intended for the pleasure of humans into a realm shared with domesticated farm animals, the austere design vocabulary for barns traditionally reflects the practical purposes of protecting harvests, sheltering work, and comforting the herds and flocks. But through this austerity we may also detect an elegance of grace and simplicity.

With the deeply engrained Puritan ethic of frugality and hard work etched into the New England culture, decorations on farm buildings were few. Indeed, before the mid-1800s decorative embellishments on New England barns might be limited to a few patterned holes cut high in the gable walls, but even these served the practical purpose of housing swallows and other birds. As one Groton, Connecticut, farmer reminisced in 1855:

> *In barns built after the old style, "swallow holes" were always to be seen. In some of these barns I have counted twenty nests at one time, all of them being occupied. A barn swarming with a multitude of such happy, innocent inhabitants, resounds with such flutterings, twitterings and gushing outbursts of song, that it seems as if every one who enters within its precincts, even if he be a confirmed hypochondriac, must forget all his troubles, and feel his heart drawn upwards to praise Him "to whom praise alone praise is due," for their cheerful melodies. . . . And, besides the pleasure we receive from their society, they, and especially the swallows, destroy during their short stay with us an innumerable multitude of insects, which is a fact of no little importance in these insectivorous times.[3]*

Most New England farmers were content with traditional austere designs for their barns (as well as their houses) through the first half of the nineteenth century, but fashions were changing. The profound influences of the industrial revolution were ushering in an era of experimentation and innovation influenced by new construction technologies, advances in the agricultural sciences, and the "Victorian" design aesthetic that favored applied decorative embellishments and picturesque settings.

By the 1840s the influential landscape architect Andrew Jackson Downing

Fig. 1-4. Six swallow holes decorate the gable of this circa 1850 barn in Tamworth, New Hampshire.

(1814–1852) argued that the architectural style of buildings reflects the moral character of the owners, just as does the fashion of their clothing. Critical of the Greek Revival style and the "common-place and meager" designs by farmers that were being published in agricultural journals, Downing suggested that the design of buildings should not be merely left to the owner or the builder but should instead follow the more "truthful" and "beautiful" designs of architects.

Through his pattern books, Downing offered fashionable designs by leading American and English architects for farmhouses in the "pointed"

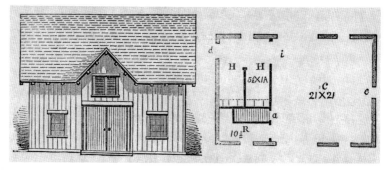

Fig. 1-5. In 1850, A. J. Downing's *The Architecture of Country Houses* offered this example of a "Model Cottage Stable" in the "simplest bracketed mode" with board-and-batten siding. The double doors on both the front and rear would allow carriages to drive in and out of the building without backing the horses. The open area at the right side of the floor plan, marked "C," is for carriages. The horse stalls are labeled "H" and the harness room "R." The stairs at "a" lead up to the hayloft. Hay would be loaded through the door in the small gable above the main entrance. Although Downing probably did not originate the design, as a leading tastemaker of the era, his endorsement helped ensure its popularity for decades.

Gothic Revival style and the "bracketed" Italian villa style. Farm stables, he suggested, "may be made to harmonize with that of the dwelling." But Downing shied away from offering farmers detailed suggestions for the design of their outbuildings. Instead, in *The Architecture of Country Houses,* first published in 1850, he provided only "a few hints, to serve those who have given it little thought, and who desire some outlines, to enable them the better to put their own ideas in a more definite shape."[4]

While the pattern books and designs of A. J. Downing and his contemporaries strongly influenced tastes in domestic architecture, especially among architects, builders, and wealthier home owners in fashion-conscious urban areas of the country, the impact on the design of barns and farm buildings was more indirect and restrained, especially in the more conservative areas of rural New England.

Fig. 1-6. The finial on the cupola and the gabled wall dormer on this utilitarian carriage barn provide hints of the Gothic Revival style. George F. Harney, architect, 1870.

Board-and-batten siding, bracketed cornices, decorative window casings, and fancy cupolas eventually found their way to some New England farm buildings, especially carriage barns, during the second half of the nineteenth century, but for most, the useful continued to dominate over beauty.

As architect J. H. Hammond warned in 1858:

> *Farmers should be put on their guard against laying out extravagant sums for the sake of making their barns "artistic" and elegant structures. They have, in general, but little capital; and this should be used for increasing the conveniences, and arrangements for the comfort of animals, rather than improving the mere outside appearance. We have contended that decorations are useless on a dwelling-house: they are utterly senseless on a barn.*[5]

Timber Frames

Stepping inside an older barn, one is immediately greeted with evidence of the technology and craft of its construction. Free of interior wall coverings, the design of the timber frame is legible, offering valuable clues about the history of the building and indeed the heritage of its makers. Even within the relatively small geographic area of the six New England states, subtle variations in the designs of barn frames may reflect evidence of the cultural history and settlement patterns of the region.

But before we explore the subtleties of barn frame designs, perhaps we should first review the terminology used to describe the basic parts of a timber frame barn.

The sills are at the bottom. These large timbers rest on the foundation and run the entire length and width of the building. Before the early twentieth century, barn footings and foundations were usually built of stone, often harvested from nearby fields or quarried from local outcroppings. Most small outbuildings and English barns had no foundations; instead the sills were laid on stone footings or "underpinnings." If the barn has a wooden floor, the timbers that support the floor boards are known as joists.

Fig. 1-7. Interior of an English barn built around 1788 in Cavendish, Vermont. Note the roof frame at the upper right with the horizontal common purlins supporting the vertically laid roof boards. At the upper left is the scaffold covered with loose boards. Rungs of a built-in ladder extend from the center post although the side rail is missing. At the right is the horizontal rail of a parapet that helps to hold the hay in the mow. At the far left is one of the large hinged barn doors. (This barn collapsed in 1988.)

In a timber frame building, large posts at the corners, along the sides, and inside support the structure and provide connections for the horizontal timbers. Posts are also sometimes incorporated into roof trusses. A simple triangular truss with a post in the center is known as a king-post truss. When two posts share the loads, it is known as a queen-post truss. Instead of a few large posts, numerous closely spaced studs support the walls of balloon-framed buildings and the platform frame construction used on most modern wood frame buildings. (See "Balloon Frames," below.)

Short diagonal braces strengthen the timber frame by keeping it from wracking. The diagonal braces that help support the rafters shown in the drawing (fig. 1-8) are known as struts. Hardwood pegs, pins, or "treenails," typically measuring an inch to an inch-and-a-half in diameter, pin the framing members together. These tapered pegs were usually hand-split from blocks of wood with a froe or hatchet and shaped with a drawknife.

Plates are the horizontal timbers at the tops of the walls that support the roof rafters. Before the first quarter of the nineteenth century, the plates on many post-and-beam frames were wider than they were tall, but square eight-by-eight-inch plates are most common afterward.

Figure 1-8 shows a frame with four pairs of principal rafters. Purlins connect the principal rafters and provide nailing for vertically laid roof boards. Often these purlins are long, tapered timbers that run the entire length of the roof in one piece. An alternative roof framing design uses numerous closely spaced common rafters to support the roof without purlins (see fig. 1-21).

The ridgepole connects the rafters at the top ridge of the roof. Although all purlin frame roofs require ridgepoles, many frames that use common rafters to support the roof lack the top timber. Instead of connecting the rafters into mortises in the ridgepole, the alternative design has the pair of rafters connecting to each other at the top with a pegged half-lap joint, and the horizontally laid roof boards provide the lateral support.

Wall girts connect the posts to provide nailing for vertically laid wall boards. Girts are also known as girders.

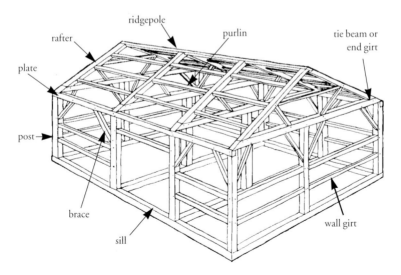

Fig. 1-8. The design of this circa 1820 English barn frame in Center Sandwich, New Hampshire, is typical of eastern New England barns cut by the scribe rule during the eighteenth and early nineteenth centuries.

The major timber that connects the bases of the rafters to form a truss is known as a tie beam, cross beam, or cross girt. This is also called an end girt when at the gable-end wall. When this beam connects the posts below the plates, it is often called a dropped girt.

Following the English tradition, in colonial New England there was a preference for timber frames to be cut from hardwood trees. As late as 1797, Samuel Deane recommended in *The Newengland Farmer or Georgical Dictionary:*

> *The sills of a barn should be made of the most durable kind of timber, as they are more liable to rot than those of other buildings, on account of the dung lying about them. White oak is very fit for this use.*[6]

As available hardwood timber resources declined, however, the use of such softwood species as spruce, pine, and hemlock became more common. Most nineteenth- and twentieth-century farm buildings have softwood frames; however, hardwood, especially oak, ash, and locust, remained the choice for pegs.

Perhaps the most obvious variation in early New England timber frame design is in roof construction. Structures built in eastern New England before the 1850s usually have their roof boards laid vertically on horizontal purlins. In western New England, however, most buildings of this era have horizontally laid roof boards on common rafters. To understand why there are such regional variations, settlement patterns and the diffusion of influence from the cultural centers of colonial New England should be considered.

In colonial New England two primary population centers developed around Massachusetts Bay and Connecticut. After immigrants from various locations in England established these colonies between the 1620s and the 1640s, a short period of inland settlement was halted by almost a century and a half of intermittent wars. As the hostilities brought relative isolation to the colonies, they gradually established their own cultural identities, based partly on the traditions brought from their English homelands and partly on the groups' own innovations, adaptations, and exposure to new influences. With the rapid expansion of settlement into the interior lands immediately after the Revolutionary War, many families (and trained builders) from Connecticut moved north to western Massachusetts and the fertile Champlain Valley of Vermont. Inland Maine, New Hampshire, and eastern Vermont, however, were settled primarily by those with roots to Massachusetts and coastal New Hampshire.

The settlers carried their regional cultural traditions of spoken language and architectural design inland through a process known to geographers as cultural diffusion.[7] Just as there are still subtle differences in the traditional pronunciations of some words between speakers in eastern and western

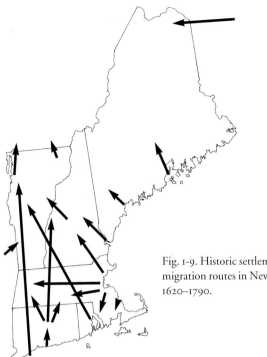

Fig. 1-9. Historic settlement and
migration routes in New England,
1620–1790.

New England, so too are there recognizable differences in the historic vernacular architecture of the two regions.[8]

The typical English barn frame built in eastern New England before the
mid-1800s, for example, has as few as four pairs of large rafters supporting
three or more purlins on each side of the roof (see fig. 1-8). Each rafter rests
on a tie beam, which rests on both the plate and the flared post. The flared
post has a mortise for the plate and a tenon for the tie beam.

In western New England, most builders of English barns traditionally
supported the roofs with numerous pairs of small, closely spaced rafters.
Roof boards were laid horizontally.

Another regional variation of late-eighteenth- and early-nineteenth-
century barn frames is in the location of the tie beams. Rather than placing
the tie beams over the plates as described above (see fig. 1-8), western New
England barn builders typically mortised the tie beams into the posts as
much as two feet below the plates. In this configuration the tie beams are
often described as dropped girts (see fig. 1-11).

Unfortunately, the posts tend to split apart at the tops with this design.
Therefore, as a repair, many barns have additional braces nailed between the
posts and the dropped girts. Other common solutions are iron or steel straps

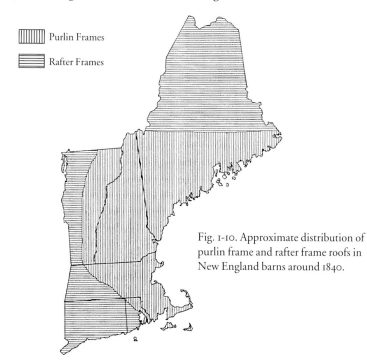

☰☰☰ Purlin Frames

≡≡≡ Rafter Frames

Fig. 1-10. Approximate distribution of purlin frame and rafter frame roofs in New England barns around 1840.

Fig. 1-11. This rare early example of a scribe rule barn frame with dropped girts was built in Cornwall, Vermont, circa 1787.

installed from the dropped girts around the outside of the posts or cables run from plate to plate.

Hand-Hewn Timbers

Before the mid-1800s, most framing timbers were hewn from tree trunks with broad axes or broad hatchets. After snapping straight lines along a face of a log with chalk or charcoal on a string, the hewer scored the surface with ax slices gauged to the proper depth. Then the excess wood was chopped away with downward swings along the length of the log. The broad ax has an offset handle to help reduce the risk of "barking" the knuckles. The broad hatchet is similar to the broad ax except that it has a smaller blade and

Fig. 1-12. Circa 1840 English barn with a hand-hewn square rule frame and rafter frame roof. The brace nailed to the face of the dropped girt at the upper left and the long plank nailed to the end girt at the far gable end are twenti-eth-century repairs. Stowe, Vermont.

Fig. 1-13. Broad hatchet.

Fig. 1-14. Timber hewn with broad ax or broad hatchet.

a shorter handle. To identify timbers hewn with a broad ax or broad hatchet, look for irregular splintered slices along the surface that follow the grain of the wood to the deep scoring cuts chopped across the grain.

After being hewn with the broad ax or broad hatchet, the rough surface of a timber was often smoothed with an adze. Shaped somewhat like a hoe (fig. 1-15), the adze is swung between the legs as the hewer straddles the timber. An adzed timber is much smoother than one hewn with a broad ax. Look for shallow scallops along the nearly flat surface.

Each joint in the timber frame required that both the mortise (the pocket into the beam) and the tenon (the protrusion that fits into the mortise) be carefully measured and cut. (See fig. 1-16.) To cut out a mortise, the timber joiner would first remove wood by boring several holes with an auger or a bit

Fig. 1-15. Adze.

Fig. 1-16. Timber hewn by a broad ax and smoothed with an adze. Note the mortise at the right.

in a bit brace. The rectangular shape of the mortise would then be cut with a large framing chisel and a mallet.

Not all barn timbers were hewn on all four sides. Small tree trunks with only one surface hewn flat often serve as roof rafters or floor joists. Sometimes the bark on the log timbers was peeled off with a drawknife or a chisel-like tool known as a spud, spudder, or barker.

A small crew of skilled timber joiners might work for several days or a few weeks to craft the frame. Only after every piece was ready would additional help be enlisted to raise the entire frame. Some sections of posts, beams, and braces would be pegged together on the ground and raised as preassembled "bents."

Fig. 1-17. Log joists support the threshing floor in this circa 1790 barn in Plymouth Notch, Vermont.

Fig. 1-18. In this barn, built circa 1790 in Plymouth Notch, Vermont, the timber frame was cut by the scribe rule. The large horizontal cross girt at the upper left and the plate beneath are supported by flared posts.

By carefully examining the design of a timber frame, it may be possible to determine how these bents were configured. Scribe rule English barns constructed before the early 1800s, for example, usually had their front and rear eaves sides constructed as bents, with the cross girts installed as separate pieces to hold the sides together (see fig. 1-8). The bents of mid-nineteenth-century square rule gable-front barns, however, typically ran parallel to the gable ends, with the plates along the eaves installed afterward. To enlarge the capacity of the barn, additional bents could be added to the rear.

Scribe Rule and Square Rule

From the first English settlement of New England through the early 1800s, timber joiners typically cut each tenon to fit a specific mortise in the frame, following a technique for making timber frames known as the scribe rule. Also known as the Latin scribe rule, the obscure origins of this framing technique date back at least to medieval Europe.

After a mortise was cut in one timber, the tenon on the joining timber would be cut. The two timbers would be brought together to adjust the fit of the joint. After being joined, the irregular shape of the receiving timber was scribed to the end of the timber being inserted. Excess wood was removed to the scribe line.[9]

After fitting, the joints on each timber would be inscribed with "marriage marks" to identify how to reassemble the frame (see fig. 1-19). These were usually located on the outside faces of the timbers, where they would not show after the barn was boarded. By carefully examining a frame produced by the scribe rule, one will typically find these Roman numeral–like marriage marks. Scribed horizontal "level lines" will often be found at two or three feet above the foundation and at twenty-four inches below the top of the plate. These lines were used to level and align the building during construction.[10]

Corner posts and side posts of scribe rule frames were usually flared at the top into "gunstocks" to allow more wood for making the pegged, mortise-and-tenon joints with the plates and tie beams. Plates, ridgepoles, and common purlins were often hewn from a single tree with a taper following the natural shape of the log. These could be as long as forty or sixty feet. Rafters, too, were sometimes tapered, with the stout end at the base.

A new technique for joining timber frames was adopted by builders during the early 1800s, inspired by the principles that were revolutionizing industrial production. Known as the square rule, this framing technique is based on a mathematical design model with interchangeable parts.[11] Rather than custom-crafting each joint by scribing each timber to another, the

Fig. 1-19. On scribe rule timber frames, marriage marks like these indicate how the precut timbers were assembled at the barn raising, circa 1790, Plymouth Notch, Vermont.

Fig. 1-20. Square rule timber frame hewn with a broad ax and adze. Note how the horizontal plate was notched away about a half an inch at the bottom to accept the measured length of the corner post. Circa 1830, Salisbury, Vermont.

Fig. 1-21. Hay barn with square rule, rafter frame roof, and sawn timbers, 1877, South Burlington, Vermont.

square rule allowed framing parts to be cut to predetermined dimensions with the aid of patterns and measurements marked with a framing square. Thus, each mortise was cut to precise dimensions.

Irregularities in the depth of a plate would be relieved at the mortises so that all posts could be cut to the same length. These shallow notches at most of the mortise joints identify a square rule frame (see fig. 1-20). Even late-nineteenth-century post-and-beam buildings with sawn framing timbers may have such notches to accommodate minor size variations.

With the shift from the scribe rule to the square rule, time was saved and the required level of skill of the workers was reduced. Instead of custom-fitting and trimming each joint, each timber would be cut to the proper dimensions, and the fit of the joints would not be tried until the raising.

Coinciding with the change from the scribe rule to the square rule was a shift toward uniform-size timbers. By the 1820s few barns were built with gunstock posts or tapered plates, as most timber framers had shifted to the square rule. Instead, posts, plates, and sills were hewn or sawn to a uniform eight-by-eight-inch or nine-by-nine-inch dimension. The diagonal braces were typically sawn to four inches by four inches.

After the mid-1800s an increasing proportion of the barns in New England were being built with sawn framing timbers. Most sawmills could handle logs only up to twenty-four feet, so long plates and sills were made by piecing together shorter sawn timbers with overlapping scarf joints.

The traditional post-and-beam timber frame continued to be used for

Fig. 1-22. At least ninety people helped erect the post-and-beam timber frame for this barn raising in North Danville, Vermont, circa 1910. Photograph courtesy of Toussaint Collection, Special Collections, University of Vermont, Bailey-Howe Library.

barns into the twentieth century, although most wooden houses had been built with the lightweight balloon or plank frames for at least fifty years. As late as 1928, farmers were advised:

> *The advantages of the timber frame are that it is strong and substantial, and many carpenters who are not familiar with the plank barn will build the timber frame. The disadvantages are that about 20 per cent more lumber is used than is necessary for strength, and the labor of erecting is greater than for the plank frame.*[12]

Balloon Frames

By the second half of the nineteenth century, as timber resources grew scarcer and the more efficient circular saw blade reduced the cost of transforming logs into lumber, the lightweight "balloon" or "plank" framing technique developed in the Midwest began to spread to New England farms. As agricultural reformer Solon Robinson of Indiana observed in his influential 1868 handbook, *Facts for Farmers:*

> *Necessity has done much for the building public by introducing to their favorable notice the balloon style of building wooden buildings—a style*

which is not well understood in the old settled and well-timbered portions of our country.[13]

Balloon framing cut construction costs by reducing the size and complexity of the design of the timbers. Just as in the factories of the era, a group effort of many small, repetitive tasks replaced the earlier handcrafting of items by skilled individuals. With hundreds of pieces cut to the same dimensions and joined by cheap nails, carpenters became more assemblers than joiners.

Fig. 1-23. Hayloft of balloon-framed, ground-level stable barn, 1944, South Burlington, Vermont.

Rather than relying on a few strong, heavy posts and beams for support, the balloon frame uses many pieces of lumber sawn two inches thick to support the walls, floors, and roofs. Heavy girders are made from two-inch-thick planks nailed together. The studs extend from the sill up the entire wall to the plate below the roof, and ledger boards nailed to the studs support the floor joists. With sheathing boards nailed horizontally or diagonally to the outside of studs, the walls become a rigid plane.

The wall studs are usually 2 x 4s or 2 x 6s. Larger (2 x 8, 2 x 10, or 2 x 12) planks are used for the joists and rafters. During the twentieth century, designers introduced lightweight trusses made of 2 x 4s or 2 x 6s for barn roof frames.

Nails

Nails provide one of the best clues to the age of barns, especially those constructed during the nineteenth century, when nail-making technology advanced rapidly. Until the last decade of the 1700s and the early 1800s, hand-wrought nails typically fastened the sheathing and roof boards on building frames. These nails were made one by one by a blacksmith or nailor from square iron rod. After heating the rod in a forge, the nailor would hammer all four sides of the softened end to form a point. The pointed nail rod was reheated and cut off. Then the nail maker would insert the hot nail into a hole in a nail header or anvil and form a head with several glancing blows of the hammer. The most common shape was the "rosehead"; however, broad "butterfly" heads and narrow L-heads also were crafted. L-head nails were popular for finish work, trim boards, and flooring.

Between the 1790s and the early 1800s, various machines were invented for making nails from bars of iron. The earliest machines chopped nails off the iron bar like a guillotine, wiggling the bar from side to side with every stroke to produce a tapered shank. These are known as type "A" cut nails. At first the heads were often made by hand, but soon machines were developed to pound a head on the end. This type of nail was made until the 1830s.

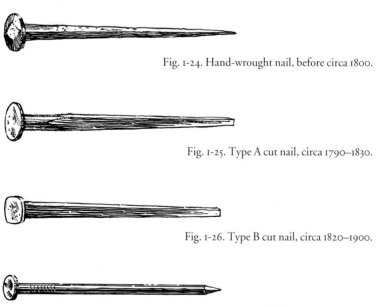

Fig. 1-24. Hand-wrought nail, before circa 1800.

Fig. 1-25. Type A cut nail, circa 1790–1830.

Fig. 1-26. Type B cut nail, circa 1820–1900.

Fig. 1-27. Wire nail, circa 1890 to present.

Fig. 1-28. Barn boards secured with "rosehead" hand-wrought nails, circa 1790, Poultney, Vermont.

By the 1820s, however, a more effective design for a nail-making machine was developed: it flipped the iron bar over after each stroke. With the cutter set at an angle, every nail was chopped to a taper. Nails made by this method are known as type "B" nails.

Cutting the nails leaves a small burr along the edge as the metal is torn apart. By carefully examining the edges for evidence of these burrs, it is possible to distinguish between the earlier type "A" nails and the later type "B" nails. Type "A" nails have burrs on the diagonally opposite edges, while the type "B" nails have both burrs on the same side. This kind of evidence can be used to establish the approximate period of construction or alteration of a building.

Type "B" cut nails continued to be the most common through the greater part of the nineteenth century. With the rapid development of the Bessemer process for producing inexpensive soft steel during the 1880s, however, the popularity of using iron for nail making quickly waned. By 1886, 10 percent of the nails produced in the United States were made of soft steel wire. Within six years, more steel-wire nails were being produced than iron-cut nails. By 1913, 90 percent were wire nails.[14] Cut nails are still made today, however, with the type "B" method. These are commonly used for fastening hardwood flooring.

Saw Marks

Although the earliest New England settlers and those pioneering in remote areas resorted to cutting boards from logs manually, with a pit saw, lumber produced by this laborious method is rarely found in New England. With the abundance of fast-flowing rivers and streams in the region, water-powered sawmills were typically among the first structures built in new settlements.

Pit-sawn lumber is more commonly found in areas that did not have access to waterpower or where slaves were used for the task. With one sawyer above and the "pitman" below, a pair of workers would use a long, two-handled ripsaw to cut along a log or timber that was set on a support frame. Lumber made in this way can be recognized by the irregular straight saw marks. The angles of the cuts and their spacing tend to vary slightly with each stroke. The work was slow. A crew might produce about six or eight boards or planks per hour.

Most farm buildings constructed before the 1850s have boards, planks,

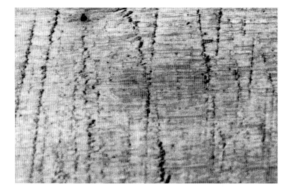

Fig. 1-29. Pit-sawn board, circa 1687, Saugus, Massachusetts.

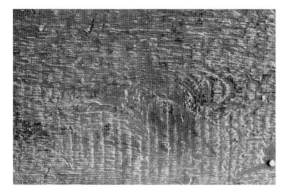

Fig. 1-30. Board sawn with sash saw before 1850, showing straight saw marks.

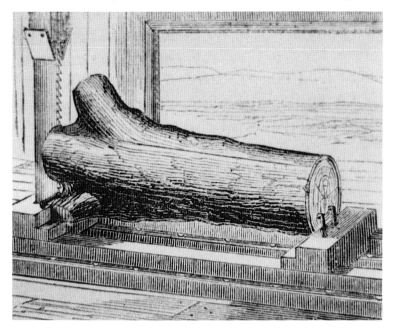

Fig. 1-31. Although by the 1850s most New England sawmills were being fitted with circular saw blades, sash saws such as this continued to be used through the late nineteenth century to cut large and irregularly shaped logs. From *American Agriculturalist,* January 1874.

and some framing lumber that were cut by water-powered sawmills equipped with sash saws. With each stroke, the coarse-toothed, reciprocating blade of the sash saw could cut about one-half to one inch of wood, leaving straight, ragged saw marks. As much as one-quarter to three-eighths of an inch of wood was wasted because of the width of the kerf left by the sash saw.

To increase productivity, the gang sash saw was developed by mounting on one frame several blades that worked together to cut the log. By the late 1800s gang sash saws with several dozen blades were used for resawing squared logs to produce many boards simultaneously.

Although a circular saw was patented in England as early as 1771, the first American "buzz" saws, with their small-diameter blades, were used for resawing lumber.[15] By the 1830s and 1840s these circular saws were being used to cut lath and clapboards. Between the 1850s and the 1870s most New England sawmills replaced their reciprocating sash saws with more efficient circular saw blades. Typically measuring from four to six feet in diameter, the coarse-toothed blades leave arc-shaped saw marks.

With the increased productivity of the sawmills equipped with circular blades, the price of lumber decreased, along with the cost of building barns.

Fig. 1-32. Circular saw marks.

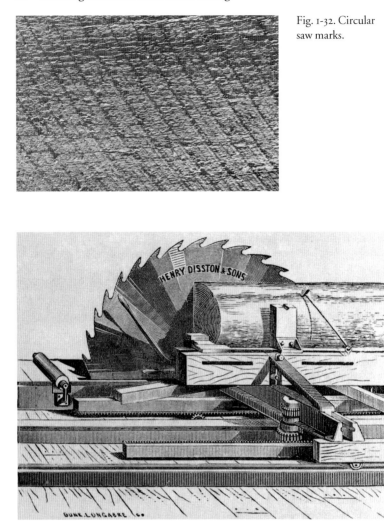

Fig. 1-33. Circular saw. From Robert Grimshaw, *Grimshaw on Saws*, 1880.

Some farmers operated their own water-powered sawmills. As one reported in 1862, "The work of construction is not great, and, thanks to our circular saws and planers, it costs but little to reduce the lumber to the proper sizes."[16] Much of the rough-sawn lumber produced by small New England sawmills is still cut with large circular saws.

By the late nineteenth century, band saws also were producing the boards and timbers used in farm buildings. The blade is a steel belt, with teeth cut along one edge, that rotates on pulleys above and below the lumber

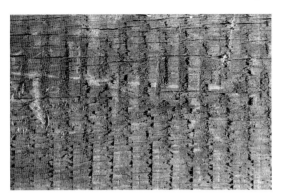

Fig. 1-34. Band saw kerf marks.

Fig. 1-35. Band saw used for resawing large timbers into boards. From Robert Grimshaw, *Grimshaw on Saws,* 1880.

being sawn. As the blade is much thinner than those of other types of saws, the width of the saw kerf is narrower, and less wood is wasted.

Early-nineteenth-century efforts to develop this technology were frustrated by the lack of high-quality steel that was both flexible and hard. By the 1870s, however, band saws were commonly used for cutting architectural scrollwork. Soon large band saws were also being installed in sawmills to resaw large timbers into boards.[17] Some mills continue to use this type of equipment.

Distinguishing between band-sawn lumber produced after the late nineteenth century and sash-sawn lumber produced before the 1850s requires careful examination. Both leave straight saw marks. The uniformly spaced marks left by band saw teeth are much finer than the coarse marks left by a sash saw, however. Band saw marks can be as close as one thirty-second of an inch. Also, band saws often leave wavy cyclical variations in the depth of the cut because of imperfections in the blade.

Wall Sheathings

Until the early 1800s the walls of most barns in New England were sheathed with rough-sawn wide boards installed vertically. Pine was very popular, although spruce, hemlock, and even chestnut were sometimes used. As the fresh lumber was typically still wet, or "green," when nailed to the outside of the frame, the boards would shrink as they dried, opening large gaps between them that would provide both light and ventilation inside the barn. When recalling how barns were built in the past, one commentator noted in 1855:

> The boards were put on without "matching" or "halving," and frequently without the use of the jointer, so that in a short time there were cracks wide and numerous enough to thoroughly ventilate the barn, and keep it cool, especially in the winter.[18]

By the 1830s and 1840s, however, New England farmers began experimenting with new methods to improve the efficiency of their barns. One inexpensive way to tighten the walls of an existing barn was to tack thin, rough boards inside, between the sheathing boards. Many barns built during this period feature two layers of vertical sheathing boards; half-inch thick, rough-sawn boards covered by inch-thick boards. Both new and existing barns also could be tightened with cedar or pine shingles. As one farmer observed in 1841:

> It is a very great and beneficial improvement in building barns to have them shingled down the sides as well as the roof; the extra expense is not so much as many people are ready to imagine, as there is considerable saving to be made in the quality of boards and nails where shingling is practiced:

besides it keeps a barn warm and the frame dry; therefore I think there is
no loss and considerable gain in the end by shingling the sides.[19]

Board-and-batten siding became a popular alternative to wooden shingles on barns during the mid-nineteenth century, especially after the development of the circular saw blade made the production of long wooden battens easier. Typically measuring about one-and-a-half to two-and-a-half inches wide and about one-and-a-quarter inches thick, these battens were nailed over the gaps between the sheathing boards (see fig. 1-38).

Although battens usually were left rough-sawn, some barn builders planed them smooth and chamfered the exposed edges. The sheathing on a large barn in Concord, Massachusetts, was described in 1854 as follows:

The outside of the barn is covered in the style known as the "Swiss fastening," that is, boards are put on extending from the brackets down, and then the joints covered with narrow, levelled strips, about two and a half inches wide. . . . The whole exterior is handsomely painted.[20]

An 1863 article in *New England Farmer* observed:

Good inch boards put on up and down and battened, are better than common siding, which is liable to split and get torn off, and is not as tight as the former way.[21]

Some farmers advocated installing double walls in the stable areas of barns. As one wrote in 1858:

Cold and open weather boarded barns can easily be made warm by boarding them up on the inside and filling up space between the outside and inside weather boarding with straw or coarse refuse hay. And this can be done at a very trifling expense by such as cannot afford to build new barns or thoroughly repair their old ones. For a few dollars worth of boards and nails and a little work, which you can do yourself, is all that is necessary to prevent the ingress of the sharp winds and cold, frosty air. And he who neglects or begrudges this is unmerciful to his poor, shivering beasts, who would soon tell him of his want of mercy if they could.[22]

By the 1860s, spruce or cedar clapboards were becoming popular for sheathing outside walls. Nailed over horizontally laid sheathing boards and typically painted with inexpensive red iron oxide paint and dressed with contrasting white trim boards, clapboards remained the most fashionable wall covering for barns, sheds, and outbuildings at least through the 1920s and 1930s.

For many farm buildings built after the 1920s, costs were reduced by

Fig. 1-36. Clapboards, circa 1870, Hinesburg, Vermont.

Fig. 1-37. Novelty siding, circa 1920, South Hero, Vermont.

sheathing the walls with tongue-and-groove boards planed with bevels to look like clapboards. This novelty siding, as it was known, was especially popular on garages, sheds, and other small farm buildings.

Such new wall coverings as asbestos cement shingles, asphalt shingles, and corrugated metal also became widespread on farm buildings in New England after the 1920s. By the 1970s many barns and farm buildings were being sheathed with plywood, especially the "T-111" type that has grooves planed into the surface about every eight inches.

Barn Doors

Prior to the 1850s, most barns had at least one pair of large hinged doors that opened onto the main drive floor. Each door measured about four or five feet wide and about eight or more feet high so that a fully loaded hay wagon could be brought inside to fill the haymow. Built of vertical boards with diagonal braces on the inside, the doors hung from large wrought-iron strap hinges. Before the machine-made wood screws became common during the mid-1800s, the door braces and hinges were fastened to the boards with wrought-iron nails that were clenched over on the inside. Machine-cut iron nails would be too brittle for clenching.

Fig. 1-38. Built in 1855 in Center Sandwich, New Hampshire, this gable-front barn with board-and-batten siding has large hinged barn doors with Z-shaped braces and a smaller pass door at the right. (Destroyed by fire in 1995.)

Large hinged doors could present problems for farmers, especially during harsh weather. An observer noted in the *New England Farmer* in 1824:

> *The large doors were towards the south, to admit the sun, when necessary, with a small door in one of the larger ones to enter when the weather is windy, and it made dangerous to open the large doors. Barns ought always to have a small door to use in the winter, when you must often be in and out.*[23]

Another farmer recalled:

> *there was usually space enough at the top and bottom of the "great barn-doors," and sometimes between them, to throw out a stray dog without injuring him in the least.*[24]

By the mid-nineteenth century a new type of door was being installed on New England barns. A convert to this method wrote in 1855:

Fig. 1-39. Interior view of a pair of well-used hinged doors on a circa 1787 English barn in Cornwall, Vermont.

Fig. 1-40. Iron wheel supporting a sliding barn door, circa 1870, Hinesburg, Vermont.

Instead of old-fashioned, double, loose, swinging, flapping doors, which, besides being inconvenient, rendered a passage into the barn absolutely dangerous in windy weather . . . each door, great and small, is now made single, or in one piece, and moves backwards and forwards so easily upon small iron wheels, that a child could with facility open or shut them.[25]

Another observer described the doors on a barn in Palmer, Massachusetts, in 1846 as follows:

Doors hung on iron rods and rollers over head, like the folding doors of the parlors of our modern houses in the cities, opening and closing with ease; made of good 1¼-inch clean stuff, and battened on the outside with open battens, formed so as to give the doors the appearance of pannel work.[26]

The tracks for these sliding barn doors could be mounted either outside or inside the front wall. Outside tracks are most common, as they were the easiest to install and would not interfere with the framing girts or hayloft floors inside. One drawback, however, is the tendency of sliding barn doors to jam or jump off the track, especially if snow and ice accumulate beneath them.

Some barns were built with large projecting hoods to help shelter the exterior door tracks from the weather and to keep snow away from the door, while others featured a simple wooden hood constructed from a few boards. Transom lights often were located above sliding doors.

Many farmers replaced the hinged doors on their older barns with sliding doors. They often left the ell-shaped wrought-iron pintles that supported the hinges in the door jambs, however.

Fig. 1-41. Pair of sliding doors mounted on an exterior track with a flared shingled hood above, circa 1850, Washington, Maine.

Fig. 1-42. Exterior sliding doors with a simple hood over the track and a transom light, circa 1890, Grafton, New Hampshire.

Fig. 1-43. The sliding main door on this circa 1860 gable-front bank barn in Rumney, New Hampshire, is mounted on an interior track. This paneled door is probably the original. The small woodshed that connects the house and the workshop with the barn has a sliding door that is hung on an exterior track. Note the small windows on the right side of the barn, which light the cow stables.

After the mid-1800s most barn doors were made of tongue-and-groove planed boards, with two or three thin layers placed diagonally or with panels set in a strong frame. To help identify the location of the barn doors at night, some farmers painted the doors white, while others decorated the doors with bold shapes.

By the late 1800s and early 1900s, haymow doors were often installed in the peak of the gable end on barns equipped with hay tracks under the ridge. These haymow doors were typically hinged or made to slide vertically.

Windows

Seventeenth- and eighteenth-century barns rarely had windows. When chores required more light than the small amount that filtered in through cracks in the walls, the doors were opened. By the early nineteenth century, however, farmers were considering ways to bring more light inside their farm buildings. One approach was to install transom lights above the main south-facing doors. In 1824, an observer noted the result with approval:

> *In passing through the country a few weeks since, I came across a barn differently constructed from any in this vicinity; and I think for neatness and convenience of construction it was superior to any I have ever seen. . . . There were twelve squares of glass arranged over the door to admit light when the large doors were shut; besides a small window in each of the gable ends, very near the ridge, for the same purpose.[27]*

Fig. 1-44. The long transom light over the doorway, the twenty-four-pane windows in the hayloft, and the ocular window at the peak of the gable help illuminate the interior of this 1860 dairy barn in Tunbridge, Vermont.

Fig. 1-45. Seven small windows mark the stalls on this circa 1870 stable in Roxbury, Connecticut.

Soon farmers were adding windows in the cow and horse stables for convenience and to improve the efficiency of their barns. An 1841 article on "proper" barn construction described how best to arrange them:

> *Another exceedingly convenient improvement is, having a number of glass windows (about six lights of 6 by 8 glass in each) in the side of the barn directly behind the cattle, which will admit the light without admitting the cold winds and storms: there is not so much danger of their getting broken as some might think, by the cattle going in and out. I have used mine two years nearly, and not a single light has ever been cracked. (The manure made by the cattle in their stalls is not thrown out of the windows, but is let down through the floor into the cellar.) There should likewise be two rows of lights over the great doors and a window in each end near the ridgepole, that is if your barn is to be 50 or 100 feet in length.*[28]

By the mid-nineteenth century the health benefits of light for their herds and flocks also were being recognized. A farmer writing in 1857 observed:

> *The light in this barn was admitted through glass windows, a decided improvement upon the* crack *system! Animals require light to be healthy.*[29]

In a discussion on barns held by the Farmers' Club in Randolph, Vermont, in 1870, a member noted:

> *All animals love the sunlight, and the more windows the better. When the sun shines; my lambs crowd together in it, and seem really to enjoy it.*[30]

The location of the cow or horse stables in a barn can often be observed by a row of small windows spaced four to six feet apart. These four- or six-pane windows are often fixed, although in some barns they are hinged or installed so that the sash can be slid open horizontally to provide ventilation.

Fig. 1-46. This fixed six-pane sash lights a mid-nineteenth-century sugar house in Hinesburg, Vermont.

Double-hung windows also have been popular for barns since the mid-nineteenth century. Typically with six-over-six sash, these windows were used for haylofts and occasionally stables. Sometimes older sash salvaged from a house renovation project would be used on farm buildings. By the 1890s two-over-two windows were being installed in some farm buildings; however, the six-over-six configuration remained popular since sashes with smaller panes were more durable and easier to repair.

By the 1920s, rows of factory-made steel or wood windows were being installed in the stables of dairy barns. Although sometimes fixed in place, often the sash could be pivoted open at the top to allow ventilation without permitting strong cold drafts, rain, or snow to blow inside.

Such farm buildings as workshops, milk houses, creameries, stables, and piggeries typically have small fixed, double-hung, casement or sliding windows with wooden sash. Late-nineteenth- and early-twentieth-century henhouses are readily identified by their large windows on the south side. Poultry barns from the 1930s and 1940s also typically have numerous windows for light and ventilation.

Foundations and Basements

Although some farmers built small cellars beneath the floors of their barns for storing vegetables to be fed to the animals through the winters, before the 1840s most barns in New England were built without basements. Instead, the sills were laid on large stones within a foot or two from the ground. The cow stables and haymow often had dirt- or clay-covered floors. As Samuel Deane recommended in 1797:

> *The sills must be laid rather low, not only for the convenient entrance of cattle and carts, but because the ground will be lowered round barns, by the yearly taking away of some of the surface with the dung. They should be well underpinned with stones laid little below the surface of the ground; and well pointed with lime, to prevent loss of manure.*[31]

Until the 1820s most barns were built without full basements. Instead, as we find in this 1824 description, small cellars were sometimes constructed as frost-free storage rooms:

> *Under the floor was a convenient cellar, in which were kept potatoes and all kinds of green vegetables for green fodder in the winter. The cellar was a very warm one, and well lighted with two windows. This cellar struck me as being the most useful apartment in the whole establishment, and I wonder that all farmers do not have one.*[32]

As late as the 1840s, the advisability of having a full basement beneath a barn was still being debated in the agricultural press. As the prolific agricultural writer and designer, Lewis F. Allen, observed of farm buildings in the *American Agriculturalist* in 1842:

> *As a general proposition . . . the building should be of wood, well framed, and covered with boards and shingles, and well set up from the ground, either on a stone walled cellar, or underpinning; usually the latter, for but a few barns or outbuildings require much cellar room.*[33]

Along the New England coast and in milder climates, cattle could graze outside throughout most of the year, and their droppings could remain to nourish the soils. But the long, harsh winters in most of New England required farmers to shelter their herds in barns for at least five months. As a result, most New England farmers faced the large task of removing manure from the stables. This was usually just shoveled outside though a small opening in the wall of the stable onto a pile near the barnyard. In newly settled

Fig. 1-47. Probably photographed in April, this mid-nineteenth-century view of a farm in Duxbury, Vermont, shows a winter's accumulation of manure piled outside the dairy barn at the left. Note the barren hills beyond. The forests were stripped for lumber and fuel and to provide grazing for sheep and then dairy cattle. Courtesy of Special Collections, University of Vermont, Bailey-Howe Library.

areas farmers often found rich virgin soils that provided good yields for several years, but those who did not return the manure to the land soon saw the fertility of the soil decline as pests and diseases ravaged their crops.

By the late eighteenth and early nineteenth centuries, most New England farmers recognized the importance of capturing all the animal waste and spreading it back on the fields so that the nutrients could be returned to fertilize their depleted soils. To prevent the leaching effects of snow and rain, some built sheds or even wooden tanks for their manure.

One of the first major innovations in barn design adopted by New England farmers between the 1830s and 1850s was the manure basement. By raising the barn onto a dry-laid stone foundation, manure could be easily collected in the basement by shoveling it through a hole in the floor. Under cover, the nutrients were protected during the long winters. If the barns were sited on sloping ground, farmers could easily remove the manure from the basement of the barn with an ox-drawn manure cart.

As one farmer thought in 1841:

> I am now confident that I save at least fifty dollars a year by keeping the manure which is made in the cellar, directly under the cattle's stall.[34]

Fig. 1-48. Bank barn with small windows lighting the stables and a manure basement below, circa 1840, Bristol, New Hampshire.

An 1853 description of a barn with a cow stable in Winchester Center, Connecticut, noted:

The manure cellar is a good method of saving the liquid and solid excre-ments on one heap without the extra expense of making tanks, &c.[35]

A visitor to a barn in Concord, Massachusetts, in 1854 reported:

I next went into the cellar; it is the whole size of the barn, and has an en-trance (sliding door) on the east side. The bottom is planked to prevent the escape of liquid manure, as the cellar was dug in sand. The manure of course occupies the south side—an immense pile. It is occasionally lev-elled, and earth and absorbents thrown on to keep it in a good state.[36]

Soon farmers were replacing their old barns with "bank barns." Others just moved their English barn onto a new stone-walled foundation to take advantage of the new space. As one farmer boasted in the *New England Farmer* in 1857:

A good cellar is as indispensable to the barn as to the house. In building one this season, we have taken care to have a full basement story, lined with pure granite walls on three sides, one front, the east, being devoted to doors and windows for entrance and light; otherwise, too, the whole is

Fig. 1-49. The *American Agriculturalist* published this design for a small side-hill barn in 1870. Note the sliding doors, board-and-batten siding, ventilator, and stone-walled basement.

ventilated. There, in the hot weather of summer, our horses, cows, pigs, and hens will be cool; and in the cold weather of winter, these, with the sheep, added at that season, will be warm.[37]

The enthusiasm was short-lived, however, as farmers soon found that the lack of ventilation and sunlight were serious drawbacks to using barn basements for sheltering some animals. By raising the main drive floor high enough to allow small windows along the basement side walls, more fresh air and light could come into the basement, which could then be used more successfully for keeping such animals as pigs and even cows through the year. An article on barn-building hints published in 1863 suggested:

The stables, which ought to be in the basement, should be arranged so as to feed from the floor above, which will save a vast amount of labor in carrying hay and straw.[38]

In 1868, farmers were told:

Place the sills upon pillars, leaving a free circulation, and space high enough to furnish shelter for all poultry in winter, and thus keep them out of the inside of the barn, where they are a nuisance.[39]

Most nineteenth-century barn basement walls are constructed of field stones. After the area for the basement had been excavated, trenches were dug around the perimeter about six or eight inches below the cellar floor level. Large flat stones were laid in the perimeter trench as the base for the stone basement walls. Where wetness could be anticipated, basement floors were often graded with a slight slope toward the outside walls. Typically, the insides of the walls were faced smooth, with field stones of various sizes projecting unevenly outward below grade. Above grade, both the inside and outside were faced. The spaces between the stones were chinked with smaller stones. Although some basement walls were finished with lime mortar, most were dry-laid.

Poured-concrete foundation walls became common during the early twentieth century, although with the development of the ground-level stable barn design, few barns were built with basements after the 1920s.

Barn basement walls are quite prone to frost damage, particularly when they are no longer used and the doors and windows are left open through the winter. Without the heat of the animals, the frost expands the soil, causing the walls to heave inward. As the walls are pushed in, the soil along the edge of the barn slumps, creating a negative slope that draws still more water into the foundation area. Soon stones work loose and the sills drop off the wall foundation, placing huge stresses on the barn frame.

Faced with eye-watering fumes, strong odors, and dampness rising from the manure in the basement, farmers' concerns over the quality of the air in-

Fig. 1-50. In this manure basement under a circa 1870 dairy barn in Brookfield, Vermont, the underpinning beneath the wall at the right has collapsed, allowing the frame of the barn to drop at least a foot.

side the barn and its effects on the health of the herd were addressed by improving the ventilation.

Cupolas and Ventilators

To reduce the amount of feed required by the animals during the winter, some farmers recommended that barns should be built with battens nailed over the cracks between the sheathing boards to reduce drafts, while others covered the walls with wooden shingles or clapboards. But farmers soon found that tight barns could lead to problems. As one observed in 1852:

> *The breath from cattle, together with the vapor arising from the manure, which defies all attempts to keep it below the floor if the cellar is warm, covers, not only the floor over the cellar, but the beams, and the whole underside of the roof, with pearly trickling drops for weeks together during the winter. If the doors are thrown open in order to evaporate this moisture, you lose the benefits you have been seeking in making a tight barn, by reducing the temperature so much that cattle require more food, while the effect is to reduce the flow of milk in the cows. . . . Many large and valuable barns have been very much damaged by being placed over a manure cellar without proper ventilation.[40]*

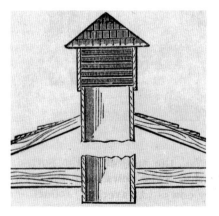

Fig. 1-51. This 1880 design for a simple louvered ventilator features a wooden air shaft that could extend down to the stable area. From *American Agriculturalist*, September 1880, 346.

The first ventilators were simple wooden louvered boxes with gable roofs, mounted near the ridge of the barn. As recognition of the importance of ventilation grew, so, as this 1855 commentary makes clear, did the size and ornamentation of the ventilators:

> *If a stranger from some removed corner of our land, where these "new-fashioned" barns have not yet made their appearance, should travel through the country . . . he would be very likely to conclude that nearly every farmer has an academy or meeting-house upon his premises; and when informed that these tasty buildings are barns, would, perhaps, show you the full dimensions of his eyes, and often exhibiting other signs of astonishment, wish to know the use of the cupolas or steeples which he saw upon their summits. And when told that the cupolas are "ventilators," would, doubtless, open his eyes still wider than before, and exclaim—"Ventilator? What good does a ventilator do upon a barn?" . . .*
>
> *A barn built in this manner is so snug and warm that some method of ventilating and purifying its atmosphere is rendered highly necessary, and accordingly an aperture has been left in the center of the top of the barn, which is covered with a cupola. In each of the four sides of the cupola, there is an opening, of the shape and size of a small window, into which venetian blinds are fitted and fastened. The cupola is ornamented, if the taste and means of the farmer acquiesce, with panels, mouldings and carvings in the Arabesque, Gothic, or some other style, the whole being painted and surrounded by a gilded vane, balls and letters, to indicate the different points of the compass.*[41]

Coinciding with the Italianate style of domestic architecture popular during the mid-nineteenth century, the room-sized cupola, embellished with decorative brackets and a copper weathervane, became a symbol of modern farming during the early Victorian era.

By the early twentieth century, prefabricated galvanized-steel ventilators were being marketed across the country. Designed to draw foul air out of

Fig. 1-52. The simple boxy ventilator on this gable-front barn in Moultonboro, New Hampshire, probably dates from circa 1850. (This barn was taken down in 1996 for erection at another location.)

Fig. 1-53. Topped by a horse and sulky weathervane, this circa 1895 Queen Anne style cupola in North Paris, Maine, is clad with wooden shingles laid in several decorative patterns.

Fig. 1-54. Produced by the Louden Machinery Company of Fairfield, Indiana, this steel ventilator is on a dairy barn built circa 1944 in South Burlington, Vermont.

the stables, enclosed wooden flues extended up inside the barn to the ventilators. In 1928 farmers were told that:

> The object of the cupola is to protect the opening of the flue from the elements, keep out birds, prevent back drafts as far as possible, and assist in drawing the foul air from the barn. The well designed steel ventilator accomplishes the objects. The home-built wooden cupola accomplishes none of these objectives satisfactorily. For any other purpose than ornamentation, the wood cupola should be replaced with the more modern steel cupola.[42]

The metal ventilators offered more efficient ventilation with less maintenance. Despite sometimes being ornamented with finials or weathervanes, they lacked the romantic feel of the wooden cupola. Instead, the factory-produced steel ventilator symbolized another step in the movement toward an industrial approach to farming.

Model Barns

By the mid-nineteenth century, farmers in New England felt the effects of competition from those who had moved to the Midwest. From the deep, rich soils, western farmers could raise grains and livestock more economically. The expanding networks of canals and then railroads made it possible to ship produce economically to major East Coast cities. In response to these pressures, many New England farmers sought to improve their situations through larger and more efficient barn designs. The *Maine Farmer* in 1857 expressed its belief that:

> *The building on the farm which requires the most study and real good judgment, to plan and to construct, is the one least thought of in this respect, and that is the barn.*[43]

Dramatically increasing costs of hired farm labor, resulting directly and indirectly from the heavy population losses of the Civil War, further stressed New England farmers and led them to develop labor saving equipment. As a

Fig. 1-55. Connected to a pulley running along an iron track beneath the ridge of the barn, this fork could lift large loads of loose hay into the hayloft by horse power. Circa 1890, East Burke, Vermont.

Fig. 1-56. Horse-powered grain thresher, circa 1890, East Burke, Vermont.

Fig. 1-57. In this photograph, taken circa 1900 in South Burlington, Vermont, a horse-powered buzz saw was being used to cut firewood. Photo courtesy of Paul Heald.

Bethlehem, Connecticut, farmer explained, commenting on what led him to invent a new type of mechanical hay-lifting equipment:

In the season of 1864, I saw that labor would be scarce and high, and if I ever wanted its help, it was then.[44]

One way to reduce the labor required for chores was to enlist the help of a horse. By driving mechanical equipment with horse-powered treadmills, farmers could replace the flail with a threshing machine or the hand-powered butter churn with a churning machine.

Although by the late nineteenth century a few large estate farms used steam-powered equipment, the full impact of the industrial revolution was not felt by most farm families until the twentieth century. Before then farmhouses were generally heated by woodstoves; kerosene lamps provided the lighting; and food and wash water were heated on the wood- or coal-fired cast iron kitchen range.

Many of these ideas for laborsaving devices and designs for "model barns" were shared through such weekly or monthly agricultural journals as the *New England Farmer,* published in Boston, and the *Maine Farmer,* published in Augusta. Many New England farmers also subscribed to the New York–based *American Agriculturalist* and *The Cultivator & Country Gentleman,* published in Albany, New York.

The journals frequently published descriptions of "model farms" on which new farming techniques or examples of innovative, laborsaving building designs were tried. These farms, which were often subsidized by wealthy owners, also became known as gentlemen's farms or estate farms. One subscriber to the *Maine Farmer* commented in 1895:

These "model barns" are all right. I look with pleasure upon them, and wish there might be more of them. But they remind me of what I heard Hon. Lewis Barker relate of a piece of work he undertook when in his prime. He had a very rough, stony lot he wished to clear. He bought a team and put the crew to work. He soon found more help was needed, so another crew was put on, and the job completed. Whatever he undertook he intended to finish. The stone was put into a good wall, and the land well plowed. He took an old neighbor out to see it, and the old gentleman, after looking over the work remarked: "Well, Esquire, a man who airns his money couldn't done that." I sometimes think it may apply to the "model" buildings I see, although there are exceptions.[45]

As the agricultural base of the region's economy waned during the late 1800s and the populations of many towns decreased as men and women left for better opportunities, a surplus of farms developed in many areas of New England. At the same time, the rapid growth of industry and commerce in

Fig. 1-58. Brook Farm in Cavendish, Vermont, is a representative example of a summer estate farm developed during the 1880s and 1890s. In this photograph, taken circa 1900, the large Georgian Revival style mansion is visible at the lower left. The line of farm buildings stretching to the right of the mansion includes a stable for saddle horses and driving horses, a small granary, an equipment shed and workshop, a hay barn, an icehouse, a piggery, and a chicken coop. The large bank barn at the right has stanchions for about thirty milk cows, stalls for work horses, a wooden interior silo, and a hayloft above. The three buildings clustered in the field near the center are a creamery and two houses for hired workers. The dirt road at the upper right leads to a maple sugar house. An apple orchard surrounded by a large stone wall is at the left, just above the mansion. Photo courtesy of George Davis and Stewart Schmidt.

the nation's urban areas produced many new jobs. The standard of living of some successful entrepreneurs, industrialists, and financiers increased dramatically. With convenient railroad connections to the major East Coast urban areas, affluent urban families seeking to escape from the heat and congestion of the cities could purchase attractive farm properties for their summer use.

While many of the New England states actively encouraged the redevelopment of existing farms by seasonal residents, towns sponsored summer "Old Home" days of activities to help lure successful family members back to their childhood homes. Indeed, some wealthy individuals did purchase the homesteads of their ancestors. With the husband often commuting from the city by train for the weekends, the wife, children, and domestic help would often move to the farm for the entire summer.

Although some built new summer houses, many adapted existing older homes for the new uses. Often the "summer people" enlarged or renovated

Fig. 1-59. The 1887 Farm Barn is one of four huge barns built at the outstanding Shelburne Farms estate of Dr. W. Seward Webb and Lila Vanderbilt Webb in Shelburne, Vermont. Stalls for eighty mules and horses were on the ground floor of the main block. An enormous hayloft, grain storage rooms, and the clock room are above. The wings provided workshops for blacksmiths, carpenters, and painters, as well as farm offices and a slaughterhouse.[46]

the farmhouses, adding plumbing, lighting, and heating systems. New outbuildings were constructed for farm functions as well as for guests and boarders.

Farm managers were often hired to care for the property and to farm the land. Neighboring farms were acquired to boost the land holdings and to provide housing for the farm managers and other workers.

Many model farm owners experimented with the latest scientific farming techniques and breeding programs to develop high-quality livestock and crops, and the summer residents often became patrons of local artistic, cultural, and charitable activities. With the downturn of the national economy associated with the Great Depression, the era of summer estate farms generally came to a close in New England by 1940.

Diversification and Specialization

With the competition from the West, many New England farm families diversified their efforts during the second half of the nineteenth century by taking on home industries and by adding a variety of crops and flocks. Specially designed buildings were constructed for many of these ventures. Granaries, corn cribs, piggeries, chicken coops, horse stables, equipment sheds, workshops, apiaries, icehouses, and maple sugar houses reflect this diversification.

Where soils and climatic conditions were favorable, New England farmers specialized in one main cash crop or product. The concentrations of surviving tobacco barns in the Connecticut River Valley of Connecticut and Massachusetts, the potato houses in Aroostook County, Maine, the cranberry screen houses in southeast Massachusetts, turf farms in Rhode Island, and the dairy barns and silos in Vermont illustrate this agricultural specialization.

As early as the 1840s and 1850s, agricultural fairs encouraged the quest for improvements and innovations in farming techniques by providing opportunities for farmers to share their achievements with others. From oxen pulls and harness racing to displays of fruits and vegetables, livestock, and equipment, these fairs offered recognition as well as much anticipated social gatherings.

By the 1870s and 1880s, state and federal programs were set up to pursue the scientific approach to farming that had been pioneered by the privately subsidized model estate farm owners. Over the next several decades the state

Fig. 1-60. This circa 1915 seed barn in South Kingston, Rhode Island, helped develop southern Rhode Island's specialization into turf growing and grass seed production during the early twentieth century.

Fig. 1-61. The main barn next to the billboard at the Great Barrington Fairgrounds in Great Barrington, Massachusetts, was built in 1855. The site was heavily damaged by a tornado in 1995.

land grant colleges and the agricultural experiment stations applied scientific research to develop improved farming practices, strains of plants, soil testing procedures, and measures for controlling diseases in plants and animals. Breeding associations were established to help improve the quality of the farmers' stock.

Even the Grange movement provided farmers and their families with important educational opportunities in addition to social and economic benefits. Part of a national fraternal movement that started in the 1870s, the Grange was open to both men and women. Members hosted special events, especially during the harvest season, such as this 1889 Dudley, Massachusetts, Grange gathering:

On Wednesday, August 21st, Dudley grange, accepted the invitation to hold a basket picnic at the farm of Mr. Cheney. From ten o'clock until noon the members and their families assembled, until their number reached two hundred, including several representatives of other granges and a few invited guests. After an hour spent visiting and viewing the farm and buildings, the call for dinner was sounded at 1 p.m.

During the grand march to music, the company had opportunity to view the table one hundred feet long, decorated with cut flowers, attractively set and burdened with the tempting fare which the farmer's wives are famous for providing.

The immense barn floor swept—one might almost say dusted—made a spacious dining hall, which was decorated with corn and golden rod the choice of host and hostess individually, for the national flower.

Following prayer by the chaplain, and singing, the dinner was served, after which an hour was given to after-dinner speaking. . . . Mrs. Allie E. Whitaker of the Farmer and Homes *testified to woman's interest in the grange throughout New England. Master D. M. Howe of the Oxford grange urged young men to make haste slowly to leave the farm, for an encounter with the great world will show them the comforts and value of farm life. . . . Master C. H. Potter of Senexet grange, Woodstock, Conn., reviewed the advantage of the grange for the farmer's family and told of the anxiety with which a farmer considers the future of his sons and daughters growing up at home. He felt the grange was deciding favorably many of these perplexing questions which popular speakers who laud agriculture omit to consider.*[47]

The Grange reached its height of popularity in New England between the 1890s and 1910s with many local chapters building or converting existing large buildings into grange halls. After a decline following World War I, the Grange grew again through the Depression years.

Many New England farms became virtual agricultural factories as farmers adopted modern scientific techniques, and equipment and laborsaving

building designs. The culmination of the gravity flow principle was the development of the huge multistoried, high-drive dairy barns and round barns by the turn of the century. An 1895 article in the *Maine Farmer* summed up the progressive spirit:

> *There was never a time in our State when there was so much inquiry upon and interest in the proper arrangement and construction of barns as is now abroad among our farmers. . . . [I]t is realized that there is money in a good barn, and that no one who purposes to put business methods into his management can afford to neglect this important attachment to his farm. Hence up and down the State, farmers are modifying and building over their ill planned structures, or are tearing them down to make room for the new and the modern.*[48]

By the 1910s and 1920s, gasoline-powered automobiles, trucks, and tractors were replacing horses for much of the transportation, plowing, and harvesting needs on New England farms. In rural areas where electric service was unavailable, some farmers also used stationary gasoline engines for pumping water, generating electricity for lighting, and other farm tasks. These gasoline engines were expensive and noisy to run. They also required regular maintenance and repairs.

Although most cities and towns had electrical service by the early twentieth century, the $2,000 to $3,000 cost per mile to extend electric lines to outlying farms left many rural New England families without electricity until the late 1930s or 1940s, when the federal Rural Electrification Administration helped finance the installation of power lines and generating facilities through local electricity cooperatives.[49]

As gasoline-powered tractors replaced horses for drawing equipment and the electric motor replaced horse-powered treadmills, the designs of New England barns changed during the early twentieth century. Rather than relying on muscles and gravity to move bulky materials, it became more efficient to build dairy barns with easily cleaned concrete-floored stables on the ground level. Baled hay could be loaded into the second story hayloft on an electrically powered conveyor belt, chopped cornstalks could be blown into huge vertical wooden or concrete silos, and manure could be removed with a mechanical gutter cleaner or the scoop of a tractor bucket. To provide the maximum volume of space in the hayloft, unencumbered by posts and beams, engineered wooden trusses were incorporated into the gambrel- or Gothic-roof designs of these twentieth-century barns.

Advances in medical research demonstrated that bovine tuberculosis could spread from infected cows through unsanitary conditions in the barn. To stem the spread of the disease, many infected herds were destroyed under the supervision of state agriculture departments and professors at the state land grant colleges. The following account reflects the severe impact of this disease:

> *In March, 1894, Mr. Darling's valuable herd of 92 cattle showed signs of tuberculosis. . . . Prof. Rich of the Vermont Agricultural College was at once summoned and tested the herd; 77 of the 92 responded unfavorably and were slaughtered, involving a loss of $3000. Subsequently the swine upon the place were found to be affected and were also killed. The grave in which these cattle were buried was 160 feet long, 4 feet wide and 6 feet deep.*[50]

Fig. 1-63. Circa 1960 corrugated metal dairy barns and concrete stave silos, New Haven, Vermont.

Fig. 1-64. Barn stew-
ardship in Waitsfield,
Vermont.

Many states and municipalities developed design codes for dairy barns
and milk handling facilities to help ensure a safe milk supply. To satisfy
these codes, separate sanitary milk rooms were added to many older barns
during the early twentieth century. These codes also required ceiling and
wall coverings, improved lighting and ventilation, and floors that could be
cleaned.[51]

In the twentieth century, romantic designs for farm buildings generally
fell from fashion as farmers sought to improve the efficiency of their agricultural operations with increasing use of manufactured building components
and functional standardized designs developed by agricultural engineers
outside the region. Just as some architects saw houses as "machines for living," so too, barns became machines for farming.

Boosted by the U.S. Department of Agriculture, equipment manufacturers, the chemical industry, and the system of university-based agricultural extension offices, the so-called green revolution was reshaping many
New England farms by the mid-twentieth century. As one popular national
magazine proclaimed in 1948:

> *The old barn is fast disappearing, and the nation's farms are in for a face-lifting. Agricultural experts hope to replace old-style barns with 5,000,000 gleaming buildings made of materials tailored to farm needs. . . . "Inefficient," say today's farm experts, pointing to the time and effort wasted in the wood-frame barn.*[52]

But not all New England farmers took the advice of the promoters. Many continued to use the barns that had served well for generations. Even some agricultural engineers admitted: "In some cases, experts point out, sturdy barns of the old type can be remodeled with new equipment to provide almost as much efficiency as a completely new metal layout."[53]

Indeed, because many resourceful farmers have adapted and remodeled their older buildings following the "make do, wear it out, use it up" tradition, New Englanders are fortunate still to have examples of the buildings that reflect the region's agrarian heritage.

Fig. 2-1. English barn, circa 1787, Cornwall, Vermont.

English Barns

For two centuries after the initial English colonial settlement, New Englanders built their barns to a standard design inherited from England with modifications made in response to the North American climate. Traditionally referred to by farmers simply as "the barn" and later as the "thirty-by-forty," these early barns, now known as English barns, typically measure about thirty feet by forty feet. They feature a simple gable roof with a pair of large hinged doors on the front eaves-side wall.

To survive and prosper through the long, harsh winters, New England farm families required a substantial building—often larger than the house —in which to stable their animals, store food for the animals and themselves, and shelter activities such as threshing grain, repairing equipment, and doing other farm work.

With the abundant timber resources, early colonists chose wooden shingles rather than thatch to cover the roofs. Also, the English tradition of sheltering the barn entrance with a small gable-roofed projection, known as a porch, was abandoned during the mid-1600s.

Light and fresh air would enter early English barns through the cracks between the sheathing boards rather than through windows. By the early 1800s, however, transom lights with glass window panes were often added above the main barn doors, along with small windows placed high in the gable ends.

English barns built before 1810 often have vertical sheathing boards fastened with hand-wrought "rosehead" nails and flared "gunstock" hardwood posts inside, while those built between 1810 and 1840 typically have machine-cut nails and uniformly dimensioned posts.

Fig. 2-2. Colonial English barn, circa 1693–1700 with later additions, Hingham, Massachusetts.

Fig. 2-3. Colonial English barn interior, Hingham, Massachusetts, showing roof construction with evidence of an original (ca. 1693) porch gable (right). The original roof boards ran horizontally, but the area filled in when the porch was removed features vertically laid roof boards.

Fig. 2-4. Circa 1810 English barn in Castleton, Vermont. The clapboards and small windows on the front are later alterations; however, most of the vertical sheathing boards are original.

Almost without exception, English barns were built as free-standing structures, oriented to provide a sheltered, sunny dooryard. As Samuel Deane advised in 1797:

Regard must be had to a situation of the barn. It should be at a convenient distance from the dwelling house, and other buildings; but as near as may be without danger of fire, if the shape of the ground permits. Too low a spot will be miry in spring and fall. Too high an eminence will be bad for drawing in loads, and on account of saving and making manures. If other circumstances permit, it may be best to place a barn in such a manner as to defend the dwelling house from the force of the coldest winds.[1]

Inside, English barns are divided into three sections: a wooden threshing floor in the center; enclosed stables for dairy cows, horses, and other farm animals on one side; and a haymow or "bay" on the other side. A waist-high parapet wall, either with an open frame or covered with boards, separates the haymow from the threshing floor in many English barns. (See fig. 1-7.)

Above the center floor is an upper hayloft, known by New England farmers as the scaffold or the rye-beams, typically reached by a ladder fixed to one of the center posts. Most scaffolds just have loose boards or saplings laid between the beams to support the hay while providing ventilation beneath. As one farmer recalled:

Fig. 2-5. Interior of a circa 1820 English barn in Hinesburg, Vermont. The cow stable is on the ground level at the left. Floors in the loft above are probably later additions.

On one side of the threshing floor of the barn were the stables for the horses and cattle and upon the other the great haymow. On the scaffold over the stables the "horse hay" was garnered, and upon the "little scaffold" over the far end of the barn floor were nicely piled the bound sheaves of wheat, rye, and barley, the butts all placed outward so as to hinder the entrance of the mice. Over the great beams were scaffolds made of round poles and pieces of waste lumber, generally, in such condition as to make a first-class man trap. On this scaffold was heaped the crop of oats, all awaiting the thrashing by the hand flail, the use of which generally began about Thanksgiving time.[2]

Until the 1820s, when mechanical threshing machines become common, grain was separated from the straw by threshing it with a flail against the barn floor. This long-handled tool was swung from overhead so that its attached wooden club would strike the grain stalks spread on the floor. Samuel Deane observed in the 1790s:

The threshing floor should be laid on strong and steady sleepers, and well supported beneath; otherwise carting in loads upon it will soon loosen it, and render it unfit for the operation of threshing. It should be made of planks, well seasoned and nicely jointed; and care should be taken it keep very tight. If it should be so open as to let grain, or any feeds, pass through, the grain will be worse than lost, as it will serve to feed and increase vermin. A layer of floor boards should therefore be laid under the planks.[3]

Fig. 2-6. Scaffold poles in a circa 1825 English barn in Bolton, Vermont.

Fig. 2-7. Threshing floor, circa 1810, Rumney, New Hampshire.

Fig. 2-7. Threshing floor, circa 1810, Rumney, New Hampshire.

After the grain was threshed, it was winnowed by tossing grain and chaff into the air, and letting the lightweight chaff drift away. English barns were often built with large doors on both front and rear to funnel a cross breeze. On some barns the rear doors opened high above the ground, but for barns built on level sites, both doorways were built with low sills so that hay wagons could be driven directly out after unloading.

Various designs for threshing floors were tried, each with its own merits. As one Maine farmer pointed out in 1823:

Indeed there are said to be some advantages in setting the floor at some distance from the ground, so that it may have some spring or elasticity, which causes the grain to thresh out with more facility. But the mode of placing barn floors practiced in some instances which have fallen within our notice, is the very worst which could be devised. We have seen them in places laid from 6 to 24 inches from the ground, affording a convenient dwelling place for skunks, woodchucks, hedgehogs, cats, puppies, weevils, worms, bugs, and other insects of all known and unknown denominations; rats, mice, chickens, and other poultry; toads, snakes, &c, &c. In this strong hold of noxious and filthy animals and animalculae, all creeping and flying things can vex, annoy and plunder the farmer, find a city of refuge, a secure asylum, and hiss or growl defiance to his attempts to dislodge them with a long handled pitch-fork or a pointed sled stake.[4]

The stable area for the cows and other cattle, often known as the cow house, was in an enclosed room either on one side of the English barn or in a shed-roofed addition, or lean-to, attached to the side or rear. A lightly framed floor overhead would support loose hay to help moderate temperature extremes and to provide additional convenient feed storage.

Samuel Deane offered these observations in 1797 about stables for the dairy herd:

> *A cow house should be in the southerly part of the barn, when it can well be so ordered. The cattle will be less pinched with the cold northerly winds. Another advantage is, that the heaps of dung thrown out on that side being in a sunny place, will be thawed earlier in the spring, so as to be fit to be carted out in season. On the north side, ice will sometimes remain in the heaps, or under them, till the last of May, or beginning of June.*[5]

Fig. 2-8. These mid-nineteenth-century wooden stanchions (left) pivot open on a treenail at the bottom to allow the cow's head to be inserted. The stanchion is then pulled up straight beside the animal's neck and fastened with a peg at the top. The wooden plank floor is pitched to drain toward the manure gutter in the foreground. Bolton, Vermont.

Fig. 2-9. Cow stable (top) in a lean-to with wooden stanchions, circa 1850, Bolton, Vermont. The animals would face left toward the haymow for easier feeding.

Acadian Barns

Although the international boundary between the United States and Canada was not established in northern Maine until 1842, when the Webster-Ashburton Treaty with Britain defined the border along the St. John River, French-speaking families, forced from Acadia (renamed Nova Scotia) by the British, settled in the northern part of Maine's Aroostook County as early as 1785.[6]

Fig. 2-10. With its distinctive additions, this Acadian English barn in St. Agatha, Maine, probably dates from circa 1790.

The barns built by the Acadians closely resemble the design of the English barns used by the English-speaking farmers in New England during this period, with the main door on the side wall and the interior divided into three spaces for the threshing floor, stables, and haymow. To accommodate larger herds, however, Acadian farmers often added distinctive shed-roofed stables along the entire rear side and hip-roofed sheds on the gable ends. With the arrival of the railroads in northern Aroostook County and the resulting potato boom of the late nineteenth and early twentieth centuries, many of these early barns were further expanded.

Extended English Barns

By the mid-1800s many farmers saw their traditional English barn as being too small, inefficient, and old-fashioned. As competition from the American West changed the economics of farming in New England, favoring larger herds and new ventures, some New England farmers built new gable-front

Fig. 2-11. The extension on the right of this circa 1800 English barn in Hingham, Massachusetts, was added around 1870.

barns, while others expanded the older barns by building lean-to additions off the sides or rear of the barn. Some added basements, while others simply lengthened the barns by adding extra bays at one end. These extended barns often have several front doors, with one opening to the original threshing floor.

A cautious observer shared his discovery of an older extended barn with the readers of *The Cultivator and Country Gentleman* in 1893:

> *This is not brought to notice because it is an ideal barn or all its features to be commended, but because its arrangement interested me, may interest others and may furnish suggestions. It struck me as having at some time been lengthened from what was originally a much shorter barn,*

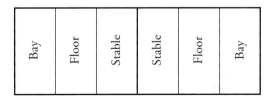

Fig. 2-12. In 1845 the *New England Farmer* offered this plan for doubling the size of a barn with an extension as "an alternative to pulling down an old barn or adding a cellar to an existing barn."[7]

the two driveways being thus accounted for and the barn's unusual length. . . .

The cattle stalls are on the south side and in the center of the building, with a close partition around them that insures perfect warmth in winter, however low the mercury may fall. The partition surrounding this space is carried to the roof, which gives two rooms over the cows that are used for poultry, one being for sitters and the other for general purposes. The whole east end of the barn is devoted to hens and hogs clear up to the "ridge-pole" even, for over the two rooms figured are two others for poul-

Fig. 2-13. The section on the left was probably added in the mid-nineteenth century to form this extended barn in Foster Center, Rhode Island.

Fig. 2-14. Around 1890 the original circa 1840 English barn was raised on a stone foundation and extended. Fairfield, Vermont.

Fig. 2-15. At least five English barns were moved end-to-end during the late nineteenth century to form this extended barn in Pawlet, Vermont.

try, reached by a stairway, and above these in the roof is a room used as a nursery for early-hatched chickens. Over the floor on the left and over the whole space in front of the cows is a flooring on which the hay is stored, as well as in the bay upon the right, the hay being driven into the barn on the floor at right where it is taken by a fork and carried wherever it is to be placed, the carrier of the hay fork running lengthwise of the barn.[8]

While most extended barns have additions grafted onto one end, extended barns could also be created by moving similarly shaped barns adjacent to each other.

Side-Hill English Barns

By the 1820s and 1830s many New England farmers were building their barns into the side of a hill to provide a frost-free manure storage area beneath the stables. The barn cellars also housed animals, especially pigs, and provided storage for farm implements. An 1823 article on barn construction observed:

Cellars to barns, under planks which are placed on sills or sleepers and form the floors of the stables or cattle stalls, are becoming fashionable in New England, are no doubt very convenient and economical.[9]

Fig. 2-16. Side-hill English barn, circa 1840, Shelburne, Vermont.

Although the gable-fronted orientation would soon become the most popular design for these "side-hill" or "bank" barns, some farmers stayed with the traditional eaves-front "thirty-by-forty" English barn design for the

Fig. 2-17. Side-hill English barn, circa 1830, Franklin, Vermont.

Fig. 2-18. This mid-nineteenth-century side-hill English barn in Newtown, Connecticut, stands on an early-twentieth-century concrete block foundation.

superstructure. Dry-laid fieldstone walls typically form three sides of the basement, with the downhill side either left open or enclosed with a wooden wall and large doors and windows. Farmers also converted older English barns into side-hill barns by moving them onto new stone foundations.

Through much of the nineteenth century, the eaves-front bank barn design remained popular for small general-purpose barns that served domestic needs with space for a horse and carriage, a milk cow, hay and oats, and perhaps some chickens or pigs. (See also "Gable-Front Barns" and "Gable-Front Bank Barns," below.)

Field Barns and Hay Barns

Rather than hurriedly carting large loads of hay from distant fields to the main barn at harvesttime, farmers often found it easier to store New England's leading crop near its source. As L. F. Allen observed in the *American Agriculturalist* in 1842:

> Some farmers, and good ones too, build small hay barns which stand scattered about their fields contiguous to springs or water courses, for storing hay as it is cut, from which it is fed out in the winter, and the cattle driven to them for that purpose.[10]

Field barns were used to store hay until it was needed during the winter. By waiting until a good snow cover, farmers often found it easier to draw

Fig. 2-19. Circa 1830 field barn in Orwell, Vermont.

Fig. 2-20. The large opening in the gable end of this circa 1830 field barn in Addison, Vermont, was added so that hay could be transferred with a horse fork.

Fig. 2-21. Early-nineteenth-century field barn, Concord, Vermont.

the hay by sled to the main barn to replace that consumed by the herd. During the second half of the nineteenth century, farmers occasionally converted their older, obsolete English barns into field barns by moving them into fields. Some of these field barns had formerly served as sheep barns during the sheep boom of the early nineteenth century.

Reconfigured English Barns

Even during the late nineteenth and early twentieth centuries, in those areas of New England where farming was still productive, obsolete English barns were often moved onto new foundations to become ground-level stable

Fig. 2-22. Two English barns hide behind the gables of this U-shaped ground-level stable barn in Richmond, Vermont. These English barns were relocated parallel to each other and connected with extensions around 1917. With easy access to the road, the top story is used mainly for hay storage. Horse stables and a granary are beneath the section closest to the road, while the other sections of the lower level at the right are lined with cow stables. The diamond patterns painted on the barn doors help farmers find the doors at night.

Fig. 2-23. Around 1910 two English barns were moved end-to-end and extended to form the hayloft above a new ground-level story added for cow stables. A single-story attached milk house is at the right. Stowe, Vermont.

barns. Often several were moved together in a line or at right angles to create a protected barnyard, sheltered from cold winter winds. Sometimes these reconfigured barns are difficult to spot as the outside walls were typically sheathed with new clapboards.

Farmers also had their older barns disassembled so that the sound timbers and boards could be reused in new structures. In these, misplaced mortises and a mixture of newer and older timbers and boards provide clues that barn was reconfigured or rebuilt.

Gable-Front Barns

Coinciding with the change to the popular gable-fronted orientation for religious and domestic architecture, New England farmers enthusiastically adopted new gable-front designs for their barns by the 1830s. Some examples in central New Hampshire date to around 1810.

The gable front offers many practical advantages. Roofs drain off to the side, rather than flooding the dooryard. With the main drive floor running

Fig. 2-24. Rear view of an early gable-front barn, reportedly built in 1810, in Rumney, New Hampshire. With large hinged doors on both the front and the rear, hay wagons could be driven straight through the barn after unloading. Near the peak of the gable is a small heart-shaped hole for birds. The companion gable-front farmhouse, also built in 1810, is seen in the distance at the left.

parallel to the ridge, the size of the barn could be increased to accommodate larger herds by adding additional bays to the rear gable end. As the *New England Farmer* recommended in 1858:

> *A barn should be at least thirty-six feet wide, with twenty feet posts. Forty-two feet wide is a better dimension. The length may be eighty feet, one hundred feet, or longer if needed. Even two hundred feet is better than three separate barns.*[11]

Several other advantages of the gable-front barn design were noted in *The Cultivator and Country Gentleman* in 1866:

The barn is 36 by 40 feet—40 east and west—the roof running north and south the shortest way of the barn. This was done in order to have the yard as wide as possible . . . and partly also to avoid a south roof, which does not last long, and would drain into the yard.[12]

Fig. 2-25. Built on grade, this early-nineteenth-century gable-front barn in Wonalancet, New Hampshire, features a shallow-pitched roof, shingled walls, and transom lights. The small door on the left leads from the cow stable, lit by the small windows behind the apple tree, to a south-facing barnyard. The offset sliding doors in front were probably installed during the late nineteenth century.

Fig. 2-26. With the side wall collapsed, this circa 1850 gable-front barn in Washington, Maine, reveals its framework. On each bent of the frame, the rafters align with the tie beams and posts. The vertically laid roof boards are supported by purlins that run between the rafters. Cedar shingles cover the roof and walls.

Many gable-front barns have the main door and drive floor offset to allow more space for the haymow on the north or west side. The narrower stables usually line the warmer south or east side, with a loft for hay or unthreshed grain above. Additional hay or grain storage was provided by the scaffolds over the drive floor.

Threshed grain was often stored in an enclosed granary room located in the barn. By the 1830s, mechanical threshing machines had generally replaced the need for threshing floors. As the improved efficiency of the grain thresher reduced the need to store the bulky unthreshed grain, the size of the mow could be reduced, and by the mid-nineteenth century many gable-front barns were built with a centered drive floor.

Gable-Front Bank Barns

Although the earliest examples of New England gable-front barns were built on grade and supported by shallow stone underpinnings, by the 1850s most new barns were built as "bank barns" on sloping sites to accommodate the increasing number of cattle in the farmers' dairy herds. This period of expansion of the dairy industry followed the sharp decline of sheep farming, especially in Vermont and Maine. Also at this time, the cost of hired farm labor increased dramatically in response to the westward migration and the Civil War. When planning their new barns, farmers sought laborsaving designs. As one writer observed in 1858: "For the Farmer there is no porter like gravitation."[13]

Fig. 2-27. With a cow stable running the entire length of the lean-to on the south side and with a manure basement beneath, this gable-front bank barn in Waitsfield, Vermont, is a typical mid-nineteenth-century dairy barn. A manure spreader stands near the left corner of the south-facing barnyard.

Fig. 2-28. View inside the gable-front bank barn in Waitsfield, Vermont, shown in fig. 2-27. The opening on the left leads to the cow stables in the lean-to addition.

Another improvement commonly made to these barns by the 1850s was the sliding barn door. By hanging the main barn door on iron or hardwood rollers that ran along a covered iron or wooden track, very large doors could be opened or closed easily, even in windy weather or after a heavy snow.

Typically two stories high, the main doorway enters on a driveway that runs the length of the main floor. Hay is piled and hoisted into mows and lofts above the main floor level. The cows are usually kept in a stable on the main floor, along with a room for grain storage. With this gable-front design, space for more cows could be created by adding additional bays to the end of the barn or by running a lean-to addition along one side. A description of a mid-nineteenth-century cow stable was published in the *New England Farmer* in 1857:

Fig. 2-29. Boxed eaves and cornice returns on the corners provided hints of the Greek Revival style on this circa 1850 gable-front bank barn in Moultonboro, New Hampshire. Remnants of a lean-to shed addition are on the left. (Demolished 1970s.)

Fig. 2-30. This beautiful circa 1850 gable-front barn in Hiram, Maine, with its boxed cornices, decorated window hoods, and sliding door, has the drive floor offset to allow larger bays for hay storage on the right side. Built on a sloping site, the manure basement is accessed at the left.

> *Mr. Wood's barn is a modern affair. The lean-to is on one side of the driveway, to which there is but one entrance, and across the one end of the barn. The cows are fastened by stanchions, and eat from the side of the barn floor. The floor under the cows was the right length to keep clean, and the ample trench received all the droppings. The walk behind the trench was tidy enough for a lady's promenade.[14]*

By the mid-nineteenth century the exterior architectural detailing of barns also became a subject of consideration. According to an 1855 article in the *New England Farmer:*

> *Among the many and recent improvements in farming matters, none is more conspicuous than the improvement in the construction of barns. . . . The gables, doors and windows of the barn are frequently orna-*

Fig. 2-31. View inside a circa 1840 gable-front bank barn in Rumney, New Hampshire, showing the stable area on the east side (*left*) and the hayloft above. (Demolished 1994.)

> *mented with pediments; and the eaves, or cornices, with wide, handsome mouldings.*[15]

Such ornamentation was previously rarely seen on the rough utilitarian barn.

Although a few barns from the 1840s and 1850s have Greek Revival style details, by the 1860s and 1870s gable-fronted dairy barns were being designed with Gothic Revival style cupolas, board-and-batten siding, and overhanging eaves with raking soffits.

Some of these barns were designed with high unobstructed spaces over the central drive floor to accommodate mechanical hay lifting devices,

Fig. 2-32. Gable-front bank barn, circa 1870, Kent's Corner, Vermont. The shift from boxed cornices to raking eaves on farm buildings coincided with transition from the Greek Revival to the Gothic Revival style of domestic architecture during the mid-nineteenth century.

Fig. 2-33. The west side (*right*) of this circa 1840 gable-front bank barn would be filled to the rafters with hay. Note the purlin frame roof of this New Hampshire barn.

Fig. 2-34. The interior of this large, circa 1870 gable-front bank barn in Brookfield, Vermont, has the feeling of a Gothic cathedral. Note that the top cross beams were cut away to allow a horse fork to run beneath the ridge of the barn roof.

known as horse forks. A Bethlehem, Connecticut, farmer, writing in 1866, described the efficacy of this arrangement:

> *The great beams, between the perline posts, were left out to facilitate get-*
> *ting up hay, a load at a time, by machinery. . . . Many times I have*
> *driven a load of hay into the barn, and in four minutes have it all to-*
> *gether, dangling in the ridge of the barn 20 feet high. Some may think this*
> *is humbug; but many a farmer can testify that it is not, having seen the*
> *load go up.*[16]

By placing the barn on a sloping site with a stone foundation beneath, a sheltered space was created where manure could easily be shoveled down through trapdoors. Protected through the winter, the manure could then be loaded into carts to return the nutrients to the soil. The barn cellars often were built with a frost-free room for storing vegetables in the winter. In 1858 an article in the *New England Farmer* wholeheartedly endorsed the barn cellar and described its contruction:

> *Upon a New England farm a good barn with a cellar under the whole is*
> *as essential as a good house with a cellar under the whole of it. . . . The*
> *walls should be made of rock pointed with mortar, with brick underpin-*
> *ning two feet high, containing, at suitable distances, small doors eighteen*
> *by sixteen inches, for the purpose of light and ventilation. The cellar*
> *should be at least eight feet deep, with two rows of brick piers eight feet*
> *apart—the whole length of the barn. The entrance for the cellar should*
> *be at one end, secured by a tight door. A barn cellar thus made will keep*
> *vegetables secure from frost in winter, and will be the proper place to store*

Fig. 2-35. Gable-front bank barn with board-and-batten siding and a cow stable ell at the right, circa 1870, Brookfield, Vermont.

Fig. 2-36. With an open basement story facing the barnyard, this late-nineteenth-century ell-shaped barn in Bradford, Vermont, is constructed of three sections, with earthen ramps leading to the two main entrances.

farming tools, carts, wheels, plows, harrows, &c. In such a cellar any quantity of manure can be made by the mixture of muck, soil, scrapings of streets, leaves and straw, with the solid and liquid manure from the oxen, cows, sheep and horses housed above.[17]

Some farmers tried stabling animals in barn basements to help protect them from the winter cold, but concerns over the quality of the air in these stables led to lively debates in the agricultural press over the merits of this practice. According to the *New England Farmer* in 1857:

A good cellar is as indispensable to the barn as to the house. In building one this season, we have taken care to have a full basement story, lined with pure granite walls on three sides, one front, the east, being devoted to doors and windows for entrance and light; otherwise, too, the whole is ventilated. There, in the hot weather of summer, our horses, cows, pigs, and hens will be cool; and in the cold weather of winter, these, with the sheep, added at that season, will be warm.[18]

The following year, the *Maine Farmer* warned:

Stables should never be in the cellar, but always above and over it. Hogs may be kept in the cellar to work over the manure. . . . Sheep should never be wintered in the cellar of a barn. The dampness is injurious to its health.[19]

These concerns were addressed by raising the main drive floor high enough to allow small windows along the basement side walls so that more ventilation and light could come into basement stables. One example was described in 1858:

> *The barn is high, with underground stalls and a stone basement. . . . The threshing floor is in the centre in which there are trap doors for the purpose of letting hay to the stalls underneath. On the right is the bay, on the left is a granary, storage room, in which is a pump, and large carriage house.*[20]

In 1863, the *New England Farmer* recommended:

> *The stables, which ought to be in the basement, should be arranged as to feed from the floor above, which will save a vast amount of labor in carrying hay and straw.*[21]

Facts for Farmers, published in 1868, also noted:

> *The stone foundation of a barn should never be laid in mortar. This is an error that should be avoided, as unnecessary and unprofitable. It would be better to place the sills upon pillars, leaving a free circulation, and space high enough to furnish shelter for all poultry in winter, and thus keep them out of the inside of the barn, where they are a nuisance.*[22]

Fig. 2-37. This turn-of-the-century gable-front bank barn with a gambrel roof has the cow stables in the basement. Colchester, Vermont.

By the late nineteenth century some New England farmers were building their bank barns with gambrel roofs. Also known as a curb roof, the double slopes of the gambrel offer more volume in the hayloft without increasing the height of the side walls. As *The Cultivator and Country Gentleman* observed in 1871:

> *Many farmers prefer the curb roof to their barns, as being more compact*

*in shape, or possessing more capacity for the exterior covering employed.
The greater height above the plates forms no objection where the pitching
is done by the horse-fork. . . . In order that the horse-fork may be used
freely, the cross-timbers above the cross-beam are entirely omitted, except
at the ends or outside.*[23]

High-Drive Bank Barns

As early as 1830 the Shaker community in Harvard, Massachusetts, was constructing a large bank barn that received great attention from the farming periodicals of the era. As the *New England Farmer* noted in 1830:

Fig. 2-38. With an extended gable that encloses the high-drive ramp, this large high-drive bank barn was built circa 1890 in Waitsfield, Vermont. The small dormer marks an interior silo.

*The Shakers of Harvard are building a barn, which, is probably larger
than any structure of the kind on this continent. The dimensions, as we
are informed, are* one hundred and fifty feet in length, and forty feet
in width. *It is four stories in height, and the calculation is to drive in on
the upper floors, from the hill-side, and pitch the hay down, thus rendering much hard labor easy.*[24]

The main innovation of this three- or four-story design was to provide access to near the top of the haymow so that loads could be dumped from wagons rather than hoisted into a loft above. The top of the main door on high-drive barns usually extends above the level of the eaves on the sides. Even when sited on steeply sloping hills, a high-drive ramp (also known as a bridge or wharfin) was often required to elevate the drive floor to the top of the hayloft. These ramps were typically built of earth and stone; however, wooden ramps were also used. A variation of this design, featuring cov-

Fig. 2-39. In this three-story high-drive barn built in 1854 by the Shaker community in Enfield, New Hampshire, the dairy herd is stabled on the lower level.

Fig. 2-40. Interior view of 1854 Shaker high-drive barn in Enfield, New Hampshire, showing the drive floor at the right and the haymow at the left.

ered high-drive ramps, is discussed in the section on "Covered High-Drive Dairy Barns."

An important early example of a multistoried, high-drive barn built on a Massachusetts estate farm was described in detail in the *New England Farmer* in 1855:

> *The barn belongs to David Leavitt, Esq., a merchant prince of New York city, who has a farm in Great Barrington, Mass., pleasantly located upon the Housatonic. It is 200 feet in length, with a centre wing on the east side, three stories high, with an arched roof covered with tin, and a cupola on the centre, and erected at an expense of nearly $20,000. It is based in a ravine which it spans, thus affording an easy entrance into the third story.[25]*

Fig. 2-41. David Leavitt's "Cascade Barn" was built in the Gothic Revival style before 1855 in Great Barrington, Massachusetts. Only the foundations of this very large structure remain. Frontispiece, *Agriculture of Massachusetts*, 1855.[25]

Fig. 2-42. The stone-walled raised yard on the right gable end provides access to the second-floor hayloft of this circa 1880 connected barn in Meredith, New Hampshire. The somewhat unusual design reflects the transition from bank barns to high-drive barns. This well-preserved local landmark takes advantage of the sloping site to locate workrooms adjacent to the kitchen in the lower level of the barn instead of in a connecting shed.

Fig. 2-43. A steep hillside provides easy access to the hayloft in this 1906 high-drive dairy barn in Cambridge, Vermont. Note the detached milk house at the right.

As the demand for butter and fluid milk increased with the advent of refrigerated railroad cars, many New England dairy farmers continued to increase the size of their herds. By the late 1880s and 1890s this growth brought another wave of barn building to the region. Led by the scientific farming approaches of the state agricultural colleges and the innovations of the Shakers and well-heeled gentlemen farmers, more and more dairy farmers invested in two-, three-, or four-story high-drive barns to minimize the labor required to move feed and manure.

The *Maine Farmer* in 1894 described New Hampshire Agricultural College's new high-drive barn:

> *There are three floors, into the first and second of which are level drive-ways, while the third floor, into which all fodder is drawn, is approached by an easy rise. This floor is thirty feet above the basement. As will be seen by the plans, the first floor is given to cows, the second to calves and sheep, while the third floor is the main driveway where all fodder is drawn in. This floor also affords room for the storage of farm implements. All fodders, when unloaded, go down instead of up, as in common barns.[26]*

Another description of a large, laborsaving barn was published in the previous year, 1893:

> *There are four floors on to which a team with load can be driven, thus saving much lifting of hay, grain, straw, etc. . . . The upper floor, or attic of the barn is reached by an easy grade made by building an embankment . . . The drive-way to the first floor . . . is bridged to secure entrance to the upper floor. . . . Twenty loads [of hay] can be run in at once and stand on this floor if such an extreme thing should be necessary in threatening weather. In unloading hay there is no pitching it up. It is dumped over the sides dropping into bays on the first floor.[27]*

Gable-front high-drive barns typically have a narrow drive floor running the length of the barn. In some, this drive has a T near the far end so that a hay wagon can be turned around inside, rather than requiring a team of horses or oxen to back out the entire length. Flanking the drive floor are open haymows that drop down a story. The cows are stabled on the middle story, and the manure is collected in the basement.

Fig. 2-44. High-drive bank barn with gambrel roof, circa 1900, Charleston, Vermont.

Fig. 2-45. Interior of a circa 1900 high-drive gambrel-roof barn in Charleston, Vermont, showing center drive floor flanked by open bays for hay. A turn-around is located at the right.

Monitor-Roofed Barns

Just as large textile mills and factories of the late nineteenth and early twentieth centuries often featured raised monitors along their roofs to provide natural light inside, some large high-drive dairy barns of the era were built with monitor roofs. In addition to the light, the monitor allows for additional ventilation, with wooden air shafts rising from the stables to louvered vents in the monitor.

The correlation between this design and the quest for improved ventilation is reflected in this 1896 description of a monitor-roofed barn in Maine:

between is the brick cattle barn, 203 feet long and 40 feet wide, 8 feet high in the walls, with monitor roof. . . rising 26 feet from the floor. This gives, for one hundred cows, 142,912 feet of air, and as, by the system of

Fig. 2-46. The design of this monitor-roofed bank barn built in 1903 in Richmond, Vermont, reflects the culmination of the gravity flow barn design. Hay was brought by horse-drawn wagons to the top story via an elevated "high-drive" ramp. Dumped into deep bays on either side of the central drive floor, the hay could then be dropped to the mangers in the cow stables on the story below. Manure, the essential by-product of dairy production, could be shoveled easily through trap doors to the basement where it was collected for distribution back to the fields. Local and state efforts are underway to help preserve this important historic agricultural landmark.

Fig. 2-47. View inside a monitor-roofed high-drive barn built in 1901 in Richmond, Vermont, showing upper drive floor and ventilation shafts leading up to the monitor.

ventilation, this is constantly changing, there is an abundance of pure oxygen every hour of the day.[28]

Although a very effective design, few monitor-roofed dairy barns were built in New England.

Covered High-Drive Dairy Barns

Perhaps the most impressive examples of nineteenth- and early-twentieth-century dairy barns are those with enclosed high-drive ramps. Some of these ramps are built with lattice trusses, much like those of the wooden covered bridges of the era. This design is found mostly in northern and western Vermont and in New Hampshire north of the White Mountains.

An early example of a large barn with a covered high-drive was described

Fig. 2-48. Covered high-drive dairy barn, built in 1888 in Waitsfield, Vermont. The concrete-floored ground-level stable is a later addition.

Fig. 2-49. Covered high-drive dairy barn, 1895, Huntington, Vermont.

Fig. 2-50. Three-story covered high-drive dairy barn, Stewartstown, New Hampshire.

Fig. 2-51. A town road passes beneath the covered high-drive on this circa 1890 dairy barn in Woodbury, Vermont. Much of this barn was rebuilt after a fire in 1903.

Fig. 2-52. Covered high-drive dairy barn with a gambrel roof and twin cupolas, circa 1900, Marshfield, Vermont.

Fig. 2-53. Side-entry high-drive barn, circa 1890, Franklin, Vermont.

Fig. 2-54. Projecting gables help shelter the two open side entrances and wharfin on this 1884 dairy barn in Georgia, Vermont.

Fig. 2-55. Inside the barn shown in fig. 2-54 is a U-shaped drive floor that would allow a team to be driven in one door and out the other after hay was unloaded in the center bay, shown here, or into haymows on the gable ends. The vertical shaft in the center draws stale air up to the cupola vent on the roof from the cow stables below .

An early example of a large barn with a covered high-drive was described in *The Cultivator and Country Gentleman* in 1867:

> *Barns with three stories are the best for saving labor. The hay is mostly pitched downward. The straw, when thrashed, is thrown downwards through shoots, or down on the tops of the stacks, out the back door. Grain from the fanning mill runs down through trap-doors into the granary bins; or is drawn off through tubes, for feeding horses and cattle below. . . . The upper floor, . . . reached through the covered bridges, . . . receives every load of hay and grain, for deposite in the bays, and when the wagons are unloaded they are driven around and out at the other door.*[29]

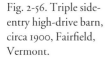

Fig. 2-56. Triple side-entry high-drive barn, circa 1900, Fairfield, Vermont.

Fig. 2-57. Built in the mid-1940s for the Vermont State Hospital, this large dairy barn in Duxbury, Vermont, featured three high-drives along one eaves side. (Destroyed by fire in 1994.)

While most covered high-drive barns have one entrance on the gable end, some were built during the late nineteenth and early twentieth centuries with one or more open or enclosed ramps entering the second-story haymow from the side wall. With two or three high-drives, teams of horses and hay wagons could be driven directly through the barn, rather than backed out. Most examples of these dairy barns are found in northwestern Vermont.

Round and Polygonal Dairy Barns

Although round barns symbolize the culmination of efficient, laborsaving designs for dairy barns of the animal-powered era of the late nineteenth and early twentieth centuries, the Shaker community of Hancock, Massachusetts, pioneered the round barn design in New England in 1826 with their Round Stone Barn.

Fig. 2-58. The monitor and cupola on the 1826 Shaker Round Stone Barn in Hancock, Massachusetts, was added in the 1870s after a fire destroyed the original wooden roof and interior.

A few other examples gathered attention in the region's agricultural press during the second half of the nineteenth century. The *Maine Farmer* published a description of an octagonal barn in Foxcroft, Maine, in 1858:

> *One of your committee a few years since changed his residence, taking a few acres of land with unfinished buildings, and wanting a barn. We decided on the octagon, but never having seen a building of that form, and no mechanic being at hand with the skill to aid us, what we did in the case is claimed as an original thing with us, and may be pertinent for the occasion, inasmuch as it may add our test of the thing to theory. . . . We are satisfied that no other disposition of the same amount of material will give so strong and spacious a structure. The frame is cheap and simple.*

Fig. 2-59. Built in 1901 in Passumpsic, Vermont, this round barn was reconstructed in 1986 at the Shelburne Museum in Shelburne, Vermont.

Fig. 2-60. Round barn, 1905, Irasburg, Vermont.

Fig. 2-61. Sixteen-sided barn with an octagonal monitor on the roof, 1906, Newbury, Vermont.

Fig. 2-62. Hayloft of a 1907 octagonal barn in Tunbridge, Vermont.

The covering, if put on as it should be takes much time. A considerable saving in labor may be made by cutting the shingles to a pattern for the corners at shop with a buzz saw and slide table. A ventilator is left at the apex of the roof, and always kept open. Good scaffold flooring can be made of plank sawed from large elm trees, which are but little worth for other purpose.

This plan, though rather on the "Chicago balloon" order in its details, is offered with much confidence.[30]

Most surviving round and multisided barns in New England, however, were built on dairy farms during the early 1900s. These later examples function similarly to the high-drive barns discussed earlier. A covered ramp leads to the top-story hayloft, cows are stabled in stanchions on the middle level, and manure storage is in the basement. In the center of some early-twentieth-century round barns is an enclosed wooden silo for storing fodder, while other round barns use the center for hay storage.

Fig. 2-63. Small octagonal barn with hipped roof, circa 1918, Ferrisburgh, Vermont.

Fig. 2-64. This 1910 twelve-sided high-drive dairy barn in Waitsfield, Vermont, with a double hipped roof, has been rehabilitated as a conference space for an inn.

A 1914 article in the *Breeder's Gazette* explained the arrangement and use of one round barn:

The round barn is beginning to have a place on some of the biggest farms in New England. J. L. Dean, of Maine, has built one that has cost less than a rectangular and he finds it more practical. . . . It is 50 feet in diameter and so arranged that the tie-up is on the outer side all around the barn, excepting an entrance on the north that enters to the feed floor. In the center on the ground floor is a concrete silo that runs to the top of the barn. There is another floor above the ground floor used as a hayloft, and the driveway to this is on the south over a concrete milkroom. . . . The animals face inward and are fed from the center of the floor and directly from the silo . . . The stock is fed with hay through individual trap doors from the hayloft, this dropping into the lower floor in front of the cattle.

The manure is taken from the tie-up in litter carriers that run around the barn on overhead tracks, passing out on to a projecting track beneath a shed, and this is dumped into a manure spreader and when filled is immediately hauled into the field. The upper floor in the hayloft is largely lighted by windows supplemented by electric lights from the universal electric plant running from a nearby city. The hay is carried in the loft by a grab fork . . . Electricity is used for power to run the different machines.[31]

Late-Nineteenth-Century Eaves-Front Bank Barns

The eaves-front design continued to be very popular for small domestic barns through the second half of the nineteenth century. Many were built for domestic use, especially when the main source of the family's income was not generated by farming. In villages, these served principally as carriage barns.

The eaves-front bank barn design also was used occasionally for some large dairy barns designed between the 1870s and around 1900, although this was not as common in New England as the gable-front bank barn de-

Fig. 2-65. Eaves-front bank barn with horse stable on the left, circa 1885, Charlotte, Vermont.

sign. On sites that allow access to the basement on a gable end, one design features a short drive floor crossing through the center of the barn, with the cow stables located on this main floor. The hay is hoisted into a loft above, and the manure drops into the basement. Later examples of these eaves-front bank barns have the dairy herd housed on. the level beneath the hayloft. These often feature two large doors on the uphill eaves side.

Fig. 2-66. With the land sloping away at the rear gable end, this large, circa 1885 eaves-front dairy barn in Cavendish, Vermont, is divided into three sections, with a drive floor in the center running between the large sliding doors on each eaves side. The rear half of the barn housed over thirty cows on the main floor, with a manure basement beneath. Box stalls for young stock were located at the near end. The barn also features a stone-walled silo in the basement, under the center drive, and an interior wooden silo on the main floor below the small gable. The arched ventilator openings in the huge cupola offer hints of the Richardsonian Romanesque architectural style.

Fig. 2-67. Interior view of the dairy barn in fig. 2-66, showing the center drive crossing with the cow stable beyond and the hayloft above.

Madawaska Twin Barns

Associated with the expansion of potato farming in the northeastern part of Aroostook County, Maine, during the early 1900s, the Madawaska twin barn has two gable-roofed or gambrel-roofed structures set parallel, with a cross gable roof between. The entrances are commonly on the eaves side. These large barns housed workhorses and various farm animals for domestic

Fig. 2-68. Madawaska twin barn, circa 1910, St. Agatha, Maine.

Fig. 2-69. Madawaska twin barn, circa 1900, Frenchville, Maine.

use. This distinctive design was probably first developed in Quebec and then adopted primarily by French-speaking potato farmers in the Saint John River valley.[32]

Ground-Level Stable Barns

By the early twentieth century the availability of mechanized power, the desire to improve sanitation, and the development of concrete as a common building material helped agricultural engineers develop a new approach to dairy barn design: the ground-level stable barn. With the discovery that the bacteria responsible for tuberculosis can pass through the digestive system

Fig. 2-70. Early ground-level stable barn with poured concrete walls on first story, circa 1920, Charlotte, Vermont.

and remain active in the airborne dust of manure, agricultural engineers sought ways to reduce the spread of the disease by improving ventilation to reduce dust levels in barns. The resulting improved barn design standards also called for increased interior light levels to help reduce bacterial growth.

As the name implies, the main floor level in a ground-level stable barn is at grade. With no manure basement, the problems of odors and disease-carrying dust in the air are greatly reduced. A four- or five-inch-thick concrete slab poured over compacted gravel typically serves as the floor for the cow stables.

Fig. 2-71. This late-nineteenth-century bank barn in Fairfield, Vermont, was converted to a ground-level stable barn with the addition of concrete floors and a mechanical gutter cleaner around 1920. Squares are scored into the concrete floor in the center aisle to improve the footing for the cows.

Fig. 2-72. Jamesway manure trolley, circa 1928, Ferrisburgh, Vermont.

Because concrete is so much easier to clean than wooden floors, sanitary regulations imposed in many areas prohibited the use of wooden floors in dairy stables. This prompted many farmers to convert manure basements in older barns into ground-level stables with concrete floors. Some older barns were jacked up and set on new first stories to allow sufficient headroom in their basements.

Separated by steel pipe stanchions, the cows are typically aligned in two rows, with elevated feeding troughs running in front of the cows. At their tail ends, a shallow gutter is recessed in the concrete to gather the manure.

Another labor-saving device that became common during the first half of the twentieth century was described in 1907:

> *The handling of the manure in modern barns is done by a trolley run on a track suspended from the ceiling in the rear passage. This track is carried through the doors at the end of the building and outside to a point where the bucket is emptied either directly into a cart or into the manure-shed, about 200 feet from the buildings.*[33]

By the mid-twentieth century many farmers had replaced their manure trolley with an electrically powered mechanical gutter cleaner. These usually required the installation of a deeper trough in the concrete floor. More recently, many of the manure gutters have been filled in to allow a small tractor to scrape the floors regularly.

With the stables occupying the entire first story, the space above serves as a hayloft. Although many early-twentieth-century examples used post-and-beam frames, by the 1920s most ground-level stable barns were being constructed with lightweight balloon frames using two-by-fours or two-by-sixes for most of the timbers. Tongue-and-groove beveled siding is common on the walls, although asbestos cement shingles also were a popular sheathing.

Fig. 2-73. Ground-level stable barn sheathed with asbestos cement shingles, 1944, South Burlington, Vermont.

Fig. 2-74. Ground-level stable barn interior showing metal pipe stanchions, concrete floor, and mechanical gutter cleaner, 1944, South Burlington, Vermont. Designed specifically for Jersey cows, the layout is unfortunately too cramped for a herd of the larger Holstein cattle now popular with dairy farmers.

Some early ground-level stable barns have concrete for the first-story walls, either poured in place or built up of cast blocks.

The gambrel roof design was universally accepted for ground-level stable barns as it enclosed a much greater volume than a gable roof did, and its shape could be formed with trusses that did not require cross beams, which would interfere with the movement and storage of hay. (See fig. 1-23.)

Fig. 2-75. Ground-level stable barn with a projecting hood over the hay track that extends from the gable peak, circa 1940, Berkshire, Vermont.

With a hay fork running along a track beneath the ridge, large loads of loose hay could be lifted from hay wagons. On some barns this hay track continues outside the gable wall beneath a triangular extension of the roof. Electric motors or gasoline engines also powered conveyer lifts to carry baled hay into the loft. When needed, the hay is dropped down from the loft through large wooden chutes or trap doors.

Single-story milk houses are typically attached to ground-level stable barns. Designed to comply with state and local ordinances intended to minimize the potential for the milk contamination, many are now fitted with large, electrically cooled stainless steel bulk storage tanks.

In the early twentieth century several midwestern manufacturers developed engineered designs for ground-level stable barns with truss-supported roofs and in addition offered metal roof ventilators, stanchions, windows, and other equipment. Two of the leading firms were the Louden Machinery Company of Fairfield, Indiana, and the James Manufacturing Company of Fort Atkinson, Wisconsin.

The ground-level stable barn with a Gothic roof uses prefabricated curved rafters to maximize the volume of the hayloft with a minimum of internal supports. Aside from the pointed arch of the roof, this design is very similar to that of dairy barns with gambrel truss roofs. A 1927 article discussed its merits:

> *The advantages of the Gothic roof, in providing a greater amount of hay space, with a given floor area, are self evident. The question of whether or not one prefers to construct this type of roof depends entirely upon whether the additional hay space is worth the extra cost. With hay chutes in each end of the barn, the labor of hay feeding is reduced to a minimum.*[34]

Fig. 2-76. Gothic-roofed ground-level stable barn with an attached milk house, circa 1925, Essex, Vermont.

Both the gambrel and the Gothic roof shapes were popular for ground-level stable barns. Examples are found in New England in areas where dairy farming continued into the twentieth century, as well as throughout other parts of North America. The ground-level stable barn design continues to be used by many dairy farmers today.

Many farmers made over their older barns into ground-level stable barns by jacking them up and adding a new story, with a concrete floor, underneath. (See fig. 2-22.) These reconfigured barns often incorporate early English barns into the complex. Although they may be difficult to spot from the exterior, they can be identified inside by the old hand-hewn post-and-beam frames.

Late-Twentieth-Century Dairy Barns

The recent shift to storing feed in silos and leaving hay outside in large round bales, or most recently polyethylene tubes, eliminates the need to store hay in dairy barns. Most ground-level stable barns and free-stall dairy barns built since the 1970s therefore have no hayloft. Instead, the roofs are supported by prefabricated wooden trusses covered with metal roofing.

While most single-story truss-roofed barns in New England are constructed with concrete foundations and stud-framed walls, pole barns with open sides are becoming popular, especially for sheltering large herds of dairy cows, heifers, and beef cattle.

Many of these large truss-roofed structures are free-stall barns, introduced in the late 1940s. They typically have concrete floors, arched superstructures of corrugated metal or truss-supported roofs, milking parlors, and open access to a yard. As an article in *Popular Mechanics* reported enthusiastically in 1948:

Fig. 2-77. Open-sided dairy barn with continuous ridge vent, circa 1980, Addison, Vermont.

Fig. 2-78. Large, open-sided, truss-roofed dairy barn, Addison, Vermont.

An experiment at the University of Wisconsin completely changes the character of the dairy barn. The experiment has proved that cows don't need stalls; that the living area of a barn needs to be cleaned only once or twice a year; and that cows in an unheated enclosure in subzero weather give as much milk as those carefully tended in a heated barn. . . . So the planners decided on the "loose housing" type of barn. In this kind of structure, much of the barn area is a big "living room" in which the cows may roam at will. The door is left open summer and winter so the cows can step outside for exercise. . . . On one end of this lounge is the "dining room" where cattle eat awaiting their turn in the "milking parlor," a separate room. Only in the parlor are stanchions provided. . . . Even the old milking stool is disappearing. Many of the new barns have "elevated cow stalls" in the milking parlor, a setup where the farmer stands in a pit so he won't have to bend over while he's milking.[35]

Many older dairy barns were adapted into free-stall barns after the 1960s by removing the stanchions inside or by constructing free-stall additions and milking parlors.

3. Outbuildings

Fig. 3-1. Wed by the connecting shed, the feminine character of this circa 1860 Gothic Revival style farmhouse with its decorative bargeboards and wraparound front porch contrasts with the more conservative design of the gable-front barn and its utilitarian dooryard. The L-shaped plan creates a large protected front yard with easy access to the road for each realm on this easterly sloping site in Center Sandwich, New Hampshire.

Connected Barns

As New England farmers countered their loss of competitive advantages during the nineteenth century by diversifying their agricultural activities and supplementing their incomes with home industries, most built small separate outbuildings clustered near the farmhouse and barn to support the various ventures. In southwestern Maine and much of New Hampshire, however, instead of constructing separate buildings, the fashion followed by most farmers was to connect the house and barn with a string of sheds and additions to contain the various spaces for work, storage, and domestic needs.

As an article in the *New England Farmer* observed in 1823:

> It is a common practice, and with many a general rule, to build the farm house adjoining, and perhaps in contact with the sheds, barns, and other out houses.[1]

Perhaps the connected barn design is best understood as a reflection of the quest to improve conditions through innovation that captured the

Fig. 3-2. In this popular ell-shaped layout, the gable-front house is connected to the English barn with a woodshed and kitchen ell to create a convenient dooryard close to the road, circa 1850, Harrington, Maine.

imaginations of nineteenth-century farmers. By rejecting traditional solutions and by taking risks and demonstrating their ideas on so-called model farms, they joined in the spirit of invention that was revolutionizing industry and consumer life. Connected architecture balanced the convenient advantages of improved access between the house and the barn against the added risks of fire.

A common arrangement is described in an article on farm buildings published in 1858 in the *Maine Farmer:*

> *The large well lighted work-shop, with sliding doors, wood-shed, piggery and henery are contained in a long building, extending across the rear of the house to the northeast corner of the barn.*[2]

The connected design continued to be popular in southwestern Maine and eastern New Hampshire throughout the nineteenth century, and farmers often moved existing outbuildings together. In his book *Big House, Little House, Back House, Barn,* Professor Thomas Hubka has delved further into the origins and motivations of this localized pattern.[3]

As late as the 1890s, connected architecture remained rare outside Maine and New Hampshire, although writers continued to praise the design, as in this 1893 description of a New England barn in *The Cultivator and Country Gentleman:*

> *A shed in which there is a watering trough . . . connects with the south and left-hand end of the barn . . . This shed connects with the house, so that the entire work of a day can be done without once setting foot out-of-doors—a convenience that means a great deal in stormy days, and days of*

Fig. 3-3. Here the barn is placed in line with the house but staggered so that the main entrances of both the barn and the house are on the gable ends, facing a road at the left and creating a sunny, east-facing side dooryard. Circa 1880, Addison, Maine.

extreme cold. The creamery is located in this shed, but separated by a partition from the space where cattle are watered.[4]

By the twentieth century the connected layout faded from popularity; concerns over fire risks and insurance costs discouraged the design.

Milk Rooms, Dairy Rooms, and Butteries

Before the 1880s, cheese and butter making were usually done on the farm. When only a small herd of cows was being milked, the milk room or dairy room was often located in an ell between the kitchen and the woodshed. Some farms had separate milk rooms and dairy rooms, while others combined the two functions in one space. In the milk room the fresh milk was

Fig. 3-4. This view of the interior of a milk room, published in the *American Agriculturalist* in 1874, shows three tiers of shelves supporting the shallow pans used to separate the cream from the milk.

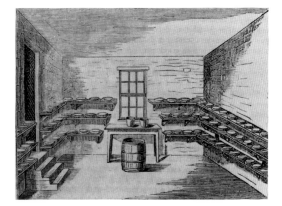

poured into shallow pans placed on shelves or racks. After the cream rose to the surface, it was skimmed off the milk and then churned to make butter. The work space where butter and cheese were made was often called the dairy room, buttery, or dairy kitchen. In 1797, Samuel Deane explained its function and importance:

> *Our farmers and their wives seem to think it necessary, or highly convenient, to have a dairy room annexed to their dwelling house, partly above and partly below ground, that they may dry their cheeses in the upper part, and set milk and cream in the lower. This, in wooden houses, is certainly not the best practice, and occasions much loss. For such an apartment will be too hot in summer and too cold in winter, to keep milk in it; neither will it be possible to keep it so sweet as it ought to be kept.*
>
> *An apartment in a cellar is better on every account to keep milk in. As to drying cheeses, it should never be kept to dry in the same room where milk is set; for they will undoubtedly communicate an acidity to the surrounding air, which will tend to turn all the milk sour that stands with the same enclosure. And a drier room would be better for cheeses; only let it be kept dark, that the flies may not come at them. So that, instead of a place called a dairy, there should be a milk room, and a cheese room, in a farm house.*[5]

Typically located off the kitchen, milk rooms were often housed in the ell near other sheltered work spaces. An especially detailed description was published in the *Maine Farmer* in 1858:

> *A few words about the kitchen and dairy rooms may be well, as they are generally considered the most important part of a farm house. The first opens from the rear of the dining room. . . . The dairy kitchen is of the same size as the main kitchen; it has conveniences for a boiler or two, and is lighted on the south side. A flight of stairs leads from this room to the ice cellar beneath, and another over them to the shed chamber; and a door opens upon the piazza or recess near the wood-shed, (this recess in front of these kitchens will be found by the farmer's wife a convenient place for drying dairy utensils, &c.) Connected with this room are a cheese room and a milk room, with windows to the north, the sash of which should be hung so as to swing either out or in, and its place in warm weather to be supplied with a wire gauze; and the doors should have shutters of the same material, to exclude insects, and at the same time admit the air freely. In the milk room are shelves on each side, and a pump and sink near the window. In the cheese room, the rows of shelves for curing cheese are in the centre of the room, with a passage between and around them, and near the window a table upon which to turn and dress it.*[6]

Creameries or Dairies

As farmers expanded the size of their dairy herds to specialize in butter production after the 1850s, some constructed a building known as the dairy, creamery, or cheese house. Often these structures were built into a bank or behind shade trees, with thick walls to help keep the proper temperature inside throughout the year. Rooftop ventilators helped to keep the buildings cool in the summer. Usually, they were heated with a wood stove vented to a brick chimney. Inside, creameries had a source of water and a sink for washing the equipment. To keep the buildings clean, the interiors were often whitewashed with lime, plastered, or finished with glazed tile.

Fig. 3-5. This circa 1885 creamery and cheese house in Cavendish, Vermont, originally had a broad wraparound porch. The workroom is at the left, and a windowless cheese storage room is at the right.

An 1874 article in the *American Agriculturalist* described a model creamery as follows:

The building should be of stone, or if of wood it should be built with at least six-inch studs, and be closely boarded with joints broken upon the studs and battened, and the inside well lathed and plastered. For thirty cows the size required would be 36 by 16 and 10 feet high, with 26 feet of it sunk four feet below the ground. In this sunken part the milk room and ice house are placed, the other portion being used for a churning room. Steps lead from the churning room down to the milk room. The ceiling is plastered, and an attic is left above to keep the rooms cool. . . . The churning is done by horse power . . . outside the building. . . . The interior of the churning room . . . contains a pump, sink, and wash bench. . . . There

*are three ranges of shelves around [the milk] room, with a table in the
center. In the winter this room is kept at a regular temperature of 60° by
means of a stove, and in the summer is cooled to the same temperature by
an inflow of cold air from the ice house which adjoins it.*[7]

Many creameries had a room for cool storage, while others were built
next to an icehouse. (See "Icehouses," below.) Some used the flow of cold
water from a spring or small stream for quickly cooling the milk in metal
tanks, the "deep setting" method of separating the cream. The amount of
time required to separate cream was greatly reduced, however, with the
adoption of centrifugal cream separators by farmers in the 1880s. The *New
England Farmer* described an up-to-date farm creamery in 1884:

*A fine large dairy house was then built, with ample storage for ice, and
all needed apparatus, such as a centrifugal cream separator, power churn,
coolers, worker, etc., etc., procured.*[8]

Fig. 3-6. Churning room of a circa 1885
creamery and cheese house in Cavendish, Vermont. Water to the sink is provided by gravity flow, using lead pipes.

Fig. 3-7. With glazed tiles covering the
floor and walls, this creamery, built
around 1900 in Acton, Massachusetts,
was set low in the ground to keep the interior sanitary and cool.

Cooperative creameries were being established throughout New England in the 1880s. Usually located next to the railroad line in villages, these
creameries processed the milk of dozens of farmers, who shipped the liquid
from the farm to the creamery by wagon in metal milk cans. In 1887 the
New England Farmer wrote in praise of this development:

*The fact that co-operative creameries have now been in operation for over
five years, and as yet there has been no failure, is the highest possible com-*

mendation of the system, and speaks volumes for the business capacity of the dairymen of New England. We look forward to the day when every agricultural town in the dairy sections of New England where butter is made shall have a cooperative creamery, managed on the cream gathering system.[9]

Icehouses

The use of ice for refrigeration became popular in New England by the middle of the nineteenth century, especially as farmers shifted to dairy production. The small farm buildings used to store ice through the summer can usually be recognized by their thick insulated walls and few windows. Early examples have low ventilators on the roof.

Often located under evergreen trees or other shady locations, many icehouses have a small entry room lit by a small window and an insulated room, connected by air ducts to the ice storage space, for storing dairy products and meats. Occasionally, brick- or stone-walled ice houses were built into a bank of earth with an entrance facing the north.

The *Cultivator* offered this advice in 1864:

A cheap Ice-House may be quickly constructed, in the form of board shanties, with a good but not tight floor. Place a few inches of sawdust on the floor, pile up the ice compactly in square blocks, leaving a space of 8 to 12 inches all around, next to the boards, to be filled with sawdust, trodden in, as the structure of ice is built upwards. Cover the whole with 8 to 10 inches of sawdust, and let plenty of fresh air blow through the shanty over the top. Ice will keep in this way as well as in the most costly

Fig. 3-8. Model icehouse illustrated in the *American Agriculturalist* in September 1880.

Fig. 3-9. Icehouse with attached shed, circa 1890, North Sandwich, New Hampshire.

Fig. 3-10. Gothic Revival style icehouse, circa 1850, Justin Morrill Homestead, Strafford, Vermont.

Fig. 3-11. This two-story brick icehouse was built in 1894 by the Shaker community in Hancock, Massachusetts, to hold about two tons of ice. On the lower level is a cold storage room for vegetables, meats, and other food.

Fig. 3-12. Shaded by large locust trees, this combined icehouse and milk house at Rokeby Museum in Ferrisburgh, Vermont, was built around 1900. The interior is divided into three spaces: the rear half is for ice storage; the door enters into a small workroom; and a refrigerated room is at the right. Note the wooden awning over the small double-sashed window that lights this insulated storage room for milk and butter.

*shanty over the top. Ice will keep in this way as well as in the most costly
and elaborate building.*[10]

*The point settled in building ice-houses is, that the whole ice-house
should be built above ground. This is the practice in Massachusetts.
There is no substance equal to a confined space of air for the walls of icehouses. Build of whatever substance you please, so that you have a double
wall, tight enough to hold air, and you will have the perfect protector of
ice. . . . Ventilation is necessary when you desire to keep food sweet. If
there is no ventilation, the confined air soon becomes very foul from animal substances on ice.*[11]

Fig. 3-13. Built on a poured-concrete foundation, this early-twentieth-century ice house on a large estate farm in East Burke, Vermont, has a small cold storage room at the left corner.

Icehouses were still being used on New England farms in the 1920s, as
this description of a Davidson, Maine, dairy farm published in 1926 reflects:

*The walls of the ice house contain an eighteen-inch air space, so that it is
unnecessary to pack the ice in either straw or sawdust. The ice is cut from
the nearest pond, and put in the icehouse, and that is all there is to it.*[12]

Icehouses continued to be used on many New England farms until electrical refrigeration was installed during the 1930s and 1940s.

Milk Houses

To help prevent the spread of tuberculosis and other diseases, state regulations developed by the early twentieth century mandated that a sanitary
milk storage room be separated from the areas where the cows were milked

Fig. 3-14. Sited next to the road, this circa 1920 milk house in Waitsfield, Vermont, has a small door at the right for loading and unloading milk cans.

Fig. 3-15. Set in a low point next to the barn, this circa 1920 milk house in West Fairlee, Vermont, originally used spring water to chill the milk; an electric compressor was installed circa 1940 for refrigeration. Note the small opening in the gable above the door for ventilation.

Fig. 3-16. This circa 1920 milk house in Charlotte, Vermont, features a steel ventilator capping its jerkin-head roof.

Fig. 3-17. Attached milk house on a 1944 ground-level stable barn in South Burlington, Vermont.

or stabled. To comply with these requirements, many New England dairy farmers added small shed-roofed or gable-roofed milk houses to their barns for storing milk. Others built small free-standing buildings, often sited in an accessible location where cold water could flow from a spring.

On most family-run dairy farms, milk houses are small gable-roofed buildings sheathed with clapboards or shingles. The door is typically on the gable end, and the side walls have small windows. Often there is a small ventilator on the roof ridge.

Inside, these buildings often have concrete cooling tubs or trenches on one side, where the cold flowing spring water would cool the milk cans. Many milk houses are built close to the road so that milk cans could be easily loaded into wagons or trucks. Some milk houses were attached to icehouses, with the ice providing refrigeration for the milk. (See fig. 3-12.)

In the 1930s and 1940s, many farmers added electrical refrigeration units to the insulated cooler rooms in milk houses. The stainless steel refrigerated bulk tank was introduced on many dairy farms by the 1960s. Rather than relying on milk cans, dairy farmers pump the milk directly into tank trucks that transport it to the dairy or creamery. To accommodate these large bulk tanks, many milk houses were replaced or expanded.[13]

Springhouses and Well Houses

Before the introduction of the electric water pump in the early twentieth century, many farms relied on springs, shallow wells, and rainwater for their water supply. These sources often fed into cisterns located underground or in the basement of the house or the barn.

Fig. 3-18. This six-sided Italianate style brick springhouse in Washington, Connecticut, probably dates from around 1860.

If the farm was fortunate to have a reliable spring located nearby at a higher elevation, the water could be fed by gravity through wooden pipes. After the 1860s, lead piping was commonly used for this purpose. To protect the source and to help keep the water free of debris, simple shelters with gable or shed roofs, rising only a few feet above the ground, were often built over the spring.

The *American Agriculturalist* offered the following suggestions in an 1874 article on springhouses:

> *The points necessary to look at most particularly in constructing a spring-house are, the coolness of the water, the purity of the air, the preservation*

Fig. 3-19. Open well house, circa 1895, on a summer estate farm in Cavendish, Vermont.

Fig. 3-20. Octagonal well house over a cistern, circa 1910, South Hero, Vermont.

Fig. 3-21. Well house, circa 1940, Brownington, Vermont.

Fig. 3-22. Springhouse, circa 1940, Fairfield, Vermont.

of an even temperature during all seasons, and perfect drainage. The first is secured by locating the house near the spring, or by conducting the water through pipes, placed at least four feet under ground. . . . The openings which admit and discharge the water, should be large enough to allow a free current of air to pass in or out. These openings should be covered with wire-gauze, to prevent insects or vermin from entering the house. The house should be smoothly plastered, and frequently whitewashed with lime, and a large ventilator should be made in the ceiling.[14]

Early springhouses and well houses usually had stone foundations, but by the twentieth century the foundations were often made of poured concrete. When the spring was conveniently located, the springhouse was often a larger building that could be used as a milk house and for cooling perishable food.

Open well houses were built to shelter dug wells or cisterns, with a bucket-hoisting apparatus or a hand pump. After the introduction of electric water pumps to most New England farms in the 1920s or 1930s, most well houses were abandoned or converted. Those that survive are more commonly found on estate farms, where they may also serve as decorative structures.

Well houses built to protect electric or gasoline-powered pumps from freezing during the winter are typically small structures with a small door or hatchway for access. They often have concrete foundation walls and are covered with a low metal roof.

Windmills

Wind-powered water pumps had become popular on farms in New England by the 1880s. With a revolving paddle blade and rudder mechanism mounted on a steel tower, the American windmill could pump water with little maintenance as long as there was a breeze. At the base is often a small shelter to protect the well head and pump mechanism. The water was typically pumped to an elevated holding tank or cistern.

Outhouses and Privies

Before the installation of indoor plumbing in farmhouses during the late nineteenth or early twentieth century, farm families relied on the outhouse, or privy. Although on farms with connected architecture the privy is typi-

Fig. 3-23. Wind-powered water pump and well house, circa 1890, Presque Isle, Maine.

Fig. 3-24. Discretely nestled between the chicken coop, icehouse, and shop is a diminutive privy, circa 1890, Ferrisburgh, Vermont.

cally located in the shed next to the woodpile between the house and the barn, separate structures are common elsewhere. These very small, gable-roofed buildings feature a hinged door. Light is provided inside by a small window located high on a wall or by a cutout in the door.

Early outhouses typically stood over pits and were moved when the space beneath was filled; later examples have metal pans or concrete bases that

Fig. 3-25. Three-holed privy, circa 1875, Grand Isle, Vermont.

could be cleaned out. The "two-holer" design allows one pile of night soil to compost before being removed.

Samuel Deane offered these observations about outhouses in 1797:

Out houses [are] slight buildings that belong to a mansion house, but stand at a little distance from it. When it can conveniently be so ordered, the out houses of a farmer ought to be so placed as to be all contiguous to the farm yard. Then all the dung, filth and rubbish they afford at any time, may be flung into the yard, without the trouble of carrying; where they will be mixed and mellowed by the trampling of beasts, and contribute to the increase of manure.[15]

Victorian era attitudes toward outhouses are reflected in this 1868 view:

Such a building should be placed convenient to the house, but never in sight. It should be located in a clump of shrubbery, mostly evergreens, out of sight from the house, or else it should be made part and parcel of some of the outbuildings, so as never to be a prominent object. We have often seen these buildings so placed that they were the most conspicuous things about the place. A very little refinement in a farmer's family will make it revolt at exposing the part of the farmery that should be hidden from public gaze.[16]

Woodsheds and Wood Houses

The firewood used for heating and cooking fuel on farms was typically stored in a woodshed attached to the kitchen, especially on farms with connected barns. As one observer wrote in 1842:

The wood-house, and milk and dairy rooms should, and usually are appended to the dwelling.[17]

For added convenience, the woodshed was often located next to the privy. Wood houses also were built as separate outbuildings, however. While those for domestic use are often sited very close to the kitchen, wood houses used for commercial purposes may be located at a site on the farm with easy access to a road. These structures may have one or more open sides or walls of wooden boards spaced widely to allow good air circulation for drying the firewood. In addition to large hinged doors, wood houses often have small

Fig. 3-26. Wood house, circa 1890, Pittsburg, New Hampshire.

Fig. 3-27. Woodshed with open bays, low-pitched shed roof, ventilators, and a raised floor, at the Shaker Village, Canterbury, New Hampshire.

openings on the walls for tossing firewood in or out. Both gable roofs and shed roofs are common.

Inside, woodsheds and wood houses usually have dirt floors littered with wood chips and pieces of bark; however, some wood houses have raised floors with ventilation beneath. Many contain a chopping block to hold the firewood as it is split with an ax or maul.

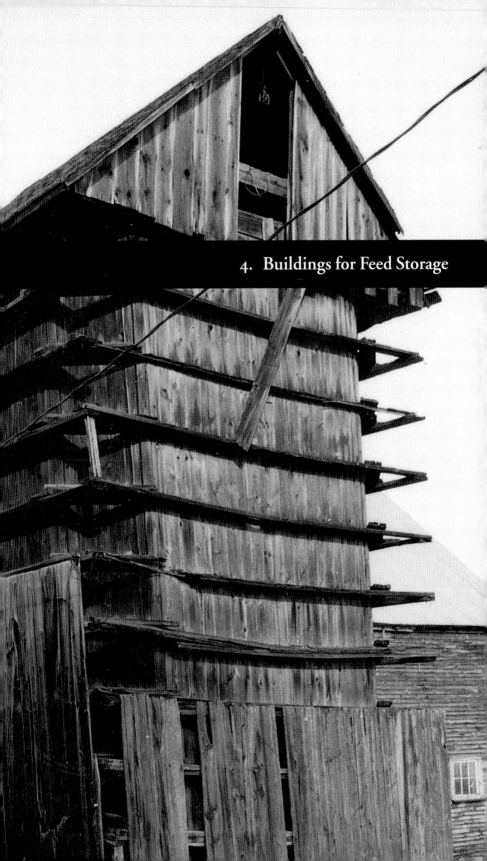

4. Buildings for Feed Storage

Fig. 4-1. This granary was built before 1740 in Hingham, Massachusetts. Inside are cribs for corn or grain sacks.[1]

Granaries

Although some New England farmers stored their threshed grain and corn in a small room in the barn, henhouse, or piggery, many built a separate storage building located next to the barn or stable. These granaries rarely have windows and are typically raised on stone corner posts and left open underneath to help keep the building dry and to discourage rodents. The door is often fitted with a lock to discourage pilferage and thievery. On granaries built to store husked corn, one wall is typically covered with vertical or horizontal wooden slats, spaced at least a half inch apart to allow abundant ventilation.

Granaries or "corn houses" were probably constructed by the earliest English settlers in New England, although few examples survive from before the nineteenth century. The following passage, published in Boston in 1797, describes the design of granaries built in New England throughout the nineteenth century:

A granary should be so constructed, that corn should be kept free of dampness, insects, and vermine. To avoid the last of these evils, its being mounted on blocks, capped with flat stones, like some of the houses for

Indian corn, is no ill expedient. But for large granaries this will not be convenient.

In granaries, where corn is to be kept for years, a very particular care should be taken in their construction. The roof should be made perfectly tight, that no rain nor snow may enter. The stories should be low, that not too much room may be unoccupied. Each floor should be covered with boxes about four feet square, leaving a passage all round between them and the outside walls, for the convenience of coming at the windows, and to prevent any wet from penetrating to the boxes. The shifting and tossing of grain from one box to another, will help to prevent or cure dampness.

To prevent the heating of corn in granaries, the windows should be opened when the air is dry, and the weather windy, but closed at other times. The grain should be laid thin at first, not more than three inches deep, and frequently stirred. After it is well dried, it may be laid in thicker heaps; or put up in casks, or sacks, as may be found convenient.[2]

Fig. 4-2. Granary constructed inside a circa 1810 barn in Rumney, New Hampshire.

Many granaries were built during the second half of the nineteenth century to store oats for workhorses. The typical granary of this era is one-and-a-half stories high with a pass door on the gable end and a loft door above. Often a beam projects from the gable. Attached to this beam is a hook for connecting a pulley to hoist grain bags into the loft. Inside, covered wooden storage bins, lined with metal, may be located on the first or second floor.

Some mid-nineteenth-century granaries have canvas chutes leading from the upper-story grain bins, with sliding wooden gates to regulate the flow of grain into a bag below. The grain was weighed on a platform balance scale.

The importance of the granary was noted in 1868:

One of the indispensable buildings of a farmery is a good storehouse for grain. Upon a small farm, a room in the barn can be set apart for the

Fig. 4-3. The left side of this circa 1850 granary at Rokeby Museum in Ferrisburgh, Vermont, serves as a corn crib with quarter-inch thick spacers between the clapboards to provide ventilation.

Fig. 4-4. View inside the second-story loft of a circa 1850 granary at Rokeby Museum in Ferrisburgh, Vermont. Note the slatted wall for storing husked corn on the left and the bins for grain at the right.

Fig. 4-5. Grain was hoisted into the upper story by connecting a pulley to the projecting ridgepole on this circa 1880 granary in Calais, Vermont.

Fig. 4-6. Circa 1900 granary on a potato farm in Monticello, Maine.

storage of small grain, but it is more liable to the depredations of rats and mice than in a building made purposefully for a granary.[3]

As this observation from 1881 reflects, granaries became even more common as grain threshing equipment was improved:

As a rule it will be found most profitable to thrash grain as soon as it has been harvested. There is a savings of time and labor in drawing the sheaves from the field directly into the thrashing machine, and moving away the straw in the barn at once. The thrashing may be done in the fields, and the straw stacked there, especially now that steam-thrashers are coming into more frequent use. When this plan becomes general, the granary will become as conspicuous a farm building as the barn. For storing the crops, it will be substituted to a great extent for the barn, and instead of the barn being a store house, it will only be a place for lodging and feeding the stock.[4]

Corn Cribs

Corn cribs were rarely built on New England farms until the middle of the nineteenth century, when growing "Indian" corn became popular. Storing the corn on the cob in well-ventilated corn cribs allowed the kernels to dry without spoiling.

The distinctively shaped corn crib, with slanted side walls built of spaced wooden slats, became common by the 1860s. The overhanging eaves and slanted walls helped prevent rain from splashing inside. Vertical side walls also are common.

Fig. 4-7. Corn crib, circa 1860, New Haven, Vermont.

Corn cribs are typically set high above the ground on wooden or stone posts. Metal pans or pie plates were sometimes laid on top of these posts to deter rats, mice, and other small animals.

Every farmer who annually raises a hundred bushels of ears of Indian corn can not afford to do without a corn-crib, because corn can not be

*stored safely except in a room with very open sides. . . . The sides should
not be less than ten feet high, and boarded up and down with strips two
inches wide, one inch apart (1868).*[6]

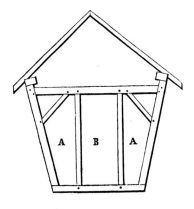

Fig. 4-8. This design for the "most improved method for framing an Indian
corn house" was published in 1862. The
sections labeled "A" are the cribs, and
the space labeled "B" is for the door and
a threshing floor.[5]

In 1881 it was observed that:

*The Connecticut corn house . . . is the common type of corn house
throughout the East. It sets upon posts covered with inverted tin pans . . .
to make it inaccessible to rats and mice. These posts are a foot or more in
diameter, and two or three feet from the surface of the ground to the bottom of the building. Sometimes flat stones, two or three feet broad, are
substituted, but the latter are preferred. The sides of the building are
made of slats nailed to sills and plates at the bottom and top, and to one
or more girders between. The bin upon the inside is made of a board par-*

Fig. 4-9. Corn crib, circa 1875, Newtown, Connecticut.

Fig. 4-10. Corn crib with vertical slatted
walls, circa 1880, Waitsfield, Vermont.

tition, three or four feet from the siding. The boards are moveable, and are put up as the crib is filled. The remaining space between the bins is used for shelling corn, or as a receptacle for bags and barrels, and the back part is sometimes used for a tool house, or fitted with bins for storing shelled corn or other grain.[7]

Interior Silos

Although the practice of storing fermented animal feed in underground pits extended back to ancient Greece and Rome, it was not until the late 1870s that wealthier New England dairy farmers began building underground storage pits for silage, often stone-lined cellars built under barns. When chopped cornstalks are compressed to prevent their exposure to the air, the silage ferments instead of spoiling. With nutritious fodder supplied to the dairy herd throughout the year, cows could be milked during the winter months.

Accounts in the *New England Farmer* and the *Maine Farmer* described barns with pit silos in 1889 and 1895:

The silos also are fitted with labor saving conveniences for filling and feeding. The silos are twenty feet deep, ten feet being of stone and cement, and ten feet more is of wood, double boarded.[8]

Fig. 4-11. Behind the typical barn clutter of stored tools and equipment is a circa 1885 interior silo. Note the tall vertical opening where small wooden panels were inserted as the silo was filled. Cavendish, Vermont.

The plan here given shows a basement extending under the main barn only fourteen feet, or but just enough to afford space for the silos.[9]

The labor required to remove the silage, however, soon encouraged the development of aboveground silos. By the 1890s, vertical wooden silos, square or rectangular in plan, were being built inside dairy barns. The corners of these square silos were often boarded at the diagonal to avoid spoilage. A small dormer was sometimes added to the roof of the barn above the interior silo; the silo could be filled to the top through the small door in the dormer. Although the use of tongue-and-groove boards was most common, some interior silos were finished inside with plaster walls.

A barn with a modern late-nineteenth-century silage operation was described in the *Maine Farmer* in 1893:

Fig. 4-12. Interior silo with plastered walls, circa 1890, Richmond, Vermont.

At the rear . . . is a cutter for cutting the ensilage for the silos. . . . This cutter is driven by an electric dynamo standing near it. It can cut one ton of ensilage corn in fifteen minutes. These three silos are each 13 x 14 and 40 feet deep. Each one holds 140 tons. They are built of wood with wooden walls clear to the ground. They are double boarded with tarred sheathing paper between.[10]

Square Wooden Silos

By the 1890s, free-standing silos were being built outside dairy barns. Among the earliest types are square wooden silos with gable roofs. These follow either of two basic designs. Some had horizontal framing members (girts) sheathed inside and out with vertical boards. Others were balloon-frame structures with long vertical studs covered with horizontal sheathing boards.

Fig. 4-13. Square silo with a gable roof, circa 1890, Waitsfield, Vermont.

Fig. 4-14. Square silo, circa 1890, Waltham, Vermont. With much of the outer sheathing missing, the horizontal framing design is revealed.

By 1906 the merits of the square silo were being seen in perspective:

The rectangular silo has been found specially adapted for being placed within a building that is in process of erection or that is already built. When wanted, partitions can be put into it at a minimum of cost, be-

cause of its shape. The objections to the rectangular as well as the square silo are, first, that difficulty has oftentimes been found in keeping the walls from spreading, and so letting air into the silage, and second, that the silage does not settle so readily in either of these forms of silo as in a round silo, hence there is more waste in the silage. Particularly is this true of the corners.[11]

Polygonal Wooden Silos

To avoid the problems with spoilage in the corners, some farmers tried eight- and ten-sided wooden silos during the early 1900s. A 1906 article weighed the merits of the approach:

The octagonal silo as the name implies is a silo with eight sides. The chief advantage gained in this form of construction, as compared with the square or rectangular silo is found in the less acute character of the angles within the same. Also from the nature of their construction, the walls are so strong that they are not liable to spread, at least not in a silo of ordinary dimensions. . . . But there are two strong objections to this form of silo. First, it is ill adapted to being placed within a building because of its shape, and second, the ventilation of the spaces within the walls is difficult because of the peculiar construction of the frame. The lining is nailed

Fig. 4-15. Octagonal wooden silo with a hipped roof, circa 1900, Milton, Vermont.

Fig. 4-16. Pair of ten-sided wooden silos with standing-seam metal roofs, circa 1900, Milton, Vermont.

onto girts rather than onto upright studs, and these girts being horizontal when in position in the wall, give rise to the difficulty mentioned. Because of these objections, it is not probable that octagonal silos will be numerously built.[12]

Stacked-Wood Silos

The structural problems presented by the framed wooden polygonal silo were avoided by constructing the walls of stacked two-by-fours. Although very rare, these stacked-wood silos were generally built around 1890 during a period of great experimentation in silo designs.

Fig. 4-17. Stacked-wood silo, circa 1890, Monkton, Vermont.

Wooden Stave Silos

Constructed much like a very large wooden barrel, with adjustable steel hoops holding the vertical grooved staves together, the round wooden stave silo was widely accepted by dairy farmers in New England from the 1890s through the 1930s. A 1906 book on silos observed that:

Fig. 4-18. Wooden stave silo, circa 1900, Pawlett, Vermont.

Fig. 4-19. Before the development of powered augers, farmers removed silage manually. Small removable wooden doors allowed access to the inside as the wooden stave silo was filled or emptied. Circa 1917, Stowe, Vermont.

> *Until within a comparatively recent period the rectangular form was usually adopted by those who built silos, but since 1890 the round silo has come so generally into favor that in a very considerable degree it is superseding the rectangular mode of construction. . . .*
>
> *Round silos can usually be built more cheaply than those that are rectangular. They have greater relative capacity, and no form of silo can be built that to so great an extent facilitates the even settling of the silage.*[13]

As one silo manufacturer proclaimed to farmers in 1908, "Square silos were of yesterday. The round silo is of today."[14]

A major producer of wooden silos in New England, the Mosely & Stoddard Manufacturing Company of Rutland, Vermont, offered "Green Mountain Silos" in either Canadian white pine or Louisiana cypress. The pine staves measured 5½ inches by 1⅞ inches, while the more durable but more expensive cypress staves measured 5¼ inches by 1¾ inches. The hoops were made from three-quarter-inch steel rod, threaded at the ends to allow adjustments in their circumference. In the fall, as the silo was filled, the hoops were loosened to accommodate the swelling of the wood as it absorbed the moisture from the silage. As the silage and wood dried, the hoops could be tightened. Removable wooden access doors extend up one side of these silos. The edges of the doors have bevels and rabbets to form an airtight seal.

Conical roofs are most common on wooden stave silos. Usually, these were originally covered with composition sheet roofing and topped with a metal ventilator. A typical twenty-four-foot-high, sixteen-foot-diameter round silo could feed a herd of about twenty-five cows for six months. The eighty-six tons of silage needed to fill this silo could be raised on about 6.4 acres.[15]

Concrete Silos

During the early 1900s some farmers experimented with poured concrete silos. Some were poured in place in forms in one piece, but the more common practice was to pour large interlocking rings that were then stacked.[16] Developed in the Midwest, the concrete silo first gained popularity in southern New England, where a popular design featured poured concrete caps.

Although the insides of these concrete silos were often painted with a bituminous paint, excessive dampness and frost penetration were seen as problems with this design, especially in northern New England, where wooden stave silos remained very popular through the 1940s.

The concrete stave silo was developed by the early 1900s. This design combines the ease of assembly of the wooden stave silo with the durability of

Fig. 4-20. Concrete silo constructed of precast rings with a conical standing-seam metal roof, circa 1930, Johnson, Vermont.

Fig. 4-21. Circular precast concrete silos with poured concrete caps, circa 1940, New Milford, Connecticut.

Fig. 4-22. Concrete stave silo, circa 1950, New Haven, Vermont.

concrete. By the 1920s various patented interlocking concrete stave designs were being produced in factories and shipped throughout the country. This soon became the most popular type of silo for New England dairy farms. Many are still in use.

As with wooden stave silos, the structures are held together with adjustable steel hoops, spaced about fifteen inches apart. Since concrete does not expand and contract with changes in moisture levels, the hoops on concrete stave silos were usually tightened only once after the structure was built. Inside, these silos are coated with a cement wash.

Tile Silos

Although occasionally used in New England, silos built of glazed tile set in cement mortar were found to be very effective for storing grass silage as they could be built nearly airtight. As was noted in 1928:

The use of tile for silos and round or curved buildings has led to the devel-

Fig. 4-23. Tile silo with a hipped roof, circa 1925, Poultney, Vermont.

opment of the curved and radially cut tile, which fit closely at the ends and form a smooth wall. . . . Silo blocks are made for 4-, 5-, and 6-inch walls. The 4-inch tile is widely used, because of ease of laying.[17]

Most of the tile silos were built during the 1920s and 1930s, but their popularity waned as the fragility of the tiles became apparent and as investment in farm structures slowed during the decline in farm prices of the Depression.

Steel Silos

Steel silos were slow to become popular with farmers in cold northern climates because of fear that the silage might freeze during the winter and spoil

Fig. 4-24. Galvanized steel silo, circa 1960, Jericho, Vermont.

more quickly. Since the 1960s and 1970s, however, steel silos have become more common on dairy farms around New England.

One contemporary silo design provides virtually airtight storage. Developed in 1945 by the A. O. Smith Company and sold under the trade name Harvestore, these shiny blue silos feature fiberglass bonded to the steel to resist corrosion and to provide insulation. Although costing nearly twice as

Fig. 4-25. Three large, dark Harvestore silos installed around the 1970s dwarf the older concrete silos on this dairy farm in New Haven, Vermont.

much as a comparable concrete stave silo, the Harvestore silos were seen as being cost-efficient because they were equipped with mechanical unloaders that removed silage from the bottom with an auger.[18]

Fig. 5-1. Circa 1870 horse stable and carriage barn with wall dormer and cupola in Redding, Connecticut.

Horse Stables and Carriage Barns

Until the 1830s, on most small farms, the horses used for riding and driving carriages were often kept in the main barn along with the other farm animals. On larger farms and in villages, however, separate stables were built for riding and carriage horses, typically with space for box stalls, carriages, harnesses, grain, and hay.

Samuel Deane provided this description of the requirements for a good stable in 1797:

A stable should have an open airy situation, and be as free as possible from mud and wetness. The floor should be built of pine planks, not on a level, but descending backwards, that the stale may not remain under the horses, so that they may lie dry and clean. As a horse is a cleanly animal, hen roosts, hog sties, and necessary houses, should not be too near to his apartment. A stable should have windows to open and shut, that fresh air may be let in when the weather is hot: And it should be tight and warm in winter. Otherwise the great vicissitudes of heat and cold will do much hurt to the animals; and the more as, being tied up, they cannot use much motion. Some of the windows should be glass, because horses are fond of light. And it is better for their eyes that they be not confined at all to total darkness in the day time. A manger is necessary in a stable, to prevent wasting of hay. . . . A box of provender may be fixed at one end of the manger, in each stall; or the manger may be made as tight as a box, to prevent loss of grain.[1]

Fig. 5-2. Small carriage house, circa 1830, Salisbury, Vermont. The elliptical opening for the door and the boxed cornice provide hints of the Federal style of architecture.

As the scale of many farm operations increased from the 1830s through the 1850s, space grew tight in the old barns, and some New England farmers built separate horse stables and carriage houses.

Early carriage houses were built just to shelter a carriage and perhaps a sleigh but not horses. The precursor to the twentieth-century garage, these outbuildings are distinguishable by their large hinged doors, few windows,

Fig. 5-3. This rare Greek Revival style brick horse stable and carriage house in Colchester, Vermont, dates from circa 1845.

Fig. 5-4. This circa 1850 open-bay barn in Georgia, Vermont, referred to as the horse barn, served as a combined horse stable, carriage barn, and workshop. Only remnants of the foundation of its companion cow barn remain nearby.

and proximity to the dooryard. Inside, they usually have wooden floors and often a workbench along one side or in the rear. The second story may have a trap door or be only partially floored so that carriages or sleighs could be hoisted aloft for storage during the off-season.

Fig. 5-5. General purpose barn with open bay, circa 1860, Brandon, Vermont.

Fig. 5-6. Carriage shed and granary (*left*), circa 1870, Tunbridge, Vermont.

Some farmers combined the horse stables with a granary, wagon shed, or farm workshop to form a multipurpose barn with a large open bay and a recessed entry. Often added during the mid-nineteenth century as farmers diversified their activities into various home industries, these free-standing structures typically have at least one large, doorless opening to allow easy access to a covered work area. This dirt-floored space could be used for repairing wagons and carriages, splitting wood, slaughtering animals, shearing sheep, or performing various other outdoor projects during inclement weather. Such open-bayed buildings could be used for the same functions as the wagon sheds described in the following section.

A design found mainly in Vermont features the recessed opening on the gable end. Elsewhere in New England it is more common to find nineteenth-century carriage sheds with the main opening on the eaves side. The *New England Farmer* described an open-bay carriage house in 1855:

> The carriage-house and horse-stables are all comprised in an L which opens upon the dooryard. Here is room to drive in several carriages and untackle, entirely protected from the weather. The common labor of "getting fixed off," must be almost wholly unknown with such conveniences.[2]

The construction of horse stables and carriage houses accelerated in New

Fig. 5-7. Carriage shed ell attached to stable, after 1849, Canterbury, New Hampshire.

Fig. 5-8. French Second Empire style horse stable, 1878, Morgan Horse Farm, Weybridge, Vermont.

England during the 1860s and 1870s as many farmers replaced their oxen with workhorses. The *Maine Farmer* noted in 1871:

> *A great many farmers who now do their work with horses, as many now do, and who also keep a horse to do their driving, are beginning to erect horse barns and carriage houses combined. They afford excellent quarters for horses, and being provided with a good hay loft, the hay suitable for horses can be selected out at haying time and put in the horse barn, instead of the main barn where it is liable from want of room to be covered up with grain, corn stalks, &c. Then there is ample room for carriages,*

Fig. 5-9. Horse stable with wall dormer, circa 1882, Cavendish, Vermont.

Fig. 5-10. Interior of circa 1882 horse stable, Cavendish, Vermont. Beaded tongue-and-groove matched boards cover the walls and ceilings.

Fig. 5-11. Horse stable and carriage house, circa 1880, Addison, Vermont.

Fig. 5-12. Circa 1880 workhorse stable (*right*) with tobacco barns beyond, East Windsor, Connecticut.

sleighs, harnesses, &c; and the former should invariably, if proper accommodations can be made at reasonable expense, occupy a room by themselves, as the odor from a stable has a tendency to corrode the varnish. The basement of such buildings—if the location admits of a basement—can be used in part as a manure receptacle, hog-stye, hen house, or for the storage of farm tools and implements. . . . The carriage room is separated from the horse stalls by a passage, and the partition is made of matched boards to completely keep out all gases from the stable. . . . Under the stairs leading to the loft at the opposite end of the passage, is a closet for brushes, curry comb, soap, oils, carriage tools and other necessary articles in use about a stable.[3]

Fig. 5-13. Village carriage barn connected to house, 1872, Center Sandwich, New Hampshire.

Fig. 5-14. Village carriage barn connected to house, circa 1880, Milbridge, Maine.

Inside, horse stables often have standing stalls or box stalls with a feed box, a manger, and a receptacle for water. Workhorse teams often stand together in eight-foot-wide double stalls. Five-foot-wide single stalls are for saddle and driving horses, and box stalls—measuring about twelve feet square—may house three or four animals or a mare and colt. In addition to a hayloft above, many larger stables also had a grain room, harness room, an area for washing and grooming, and quarters for hired help, as well as an area to store carriages and sleighs. An example of such a stable was described in the *New England Farmer* in 1884:

> *The horse stable, and carriage rooms are finished in dressed lumber, shellac varnished, and are easily kept by the attendant, who has a nicely furnished sleeping room in the building. Five driving horses are kept here, but the heavier ones are frequently used when needed at farm work. The regular farm team consists of two pairs of horses, and three yokes of oxen, kept in the farm barn.*[4]

Fig. 5-15. Small carriage shed, 1880, Charlotte, Vermont.

The combined horse stable and carriage house continued to be a common farm building through the second half of the nineteenth century and the first decade of the twentieth century. Although many New England farmers continued to house their horses in the same barn as their cows, separate horse stables were often built on potato farms and tobacco farms.

Some of the most elaborate stables and coach barns were built during the early twentieth century on horse farms and summer estate farms. Until automobiles became common, many village homes had a small stable and carriage house. As this 1928 observation on farm buildings illustrates, horse barns continued in use until tractors were adopted in the 1930s and 1940s:

The horse barn on most farms is an item of expense for maintaining work animals, rather than a factory for farm production, for which reason it is likely to be slighted, in an attempt to keep expenses as low as possible.[5]

Wagon Sheds

Known as wagon sheds, cart houses, and implement shelters, these open-bay structures protect farm vehicles and equipment from the weather and provide shelter for doing small repairs and maintenance. Although on some farms just one building served as both a wagon shed and a carriage house (see figs. 5-4, 5-5, and 5-6), many farms had separate structures for domestic and agricultural vehicles. Generally, the carriage barns have large doors and wooden floors, while the wagon sheds have open bays and dirt floors. Nineteenth-century examples typically feature hand-hewn timber frames with braced front posts. Recycled timbers and boards are common in these utilitarian farmyard buildings.

Fig. 5-16. Wagon shed, circa 1870, Waitsfield, Vermont.

Fig. 5-17. Three-bay wagon shed, circa 1880, Waitsfield, Vermont.

Distinguished by the long shed or gable roof and the row of large openings along the eaves side, the typical wagon shed was often built as a separate structure or as a wing connected to the farmhouse or the barn. As the *New England Farmer* suggested in 1863:

> *It is also a good plan to have a room, either in the basement or on the floor, for storing farm implements, such as ploughs, harrows, hay-racks, and all other tools when not in use. The better way is to have a building for that purpose.*[6]

With the mechanization of farming practices during the late nineteenth and early twentieth centuries, farmers invested in a variety of new implements and mechanical equipment. While the plows, disk harrows, spring tooth harrows, planters, cultivators, rakes, tedders, mowers, potato pickers,

Fig. 5-18. Equipment shed, circa 1930, Gray, Maine.

Fig. 5-19. Equipment shed and farm garage with concrete block walls, circa 1950, New Milford, Connecticut.

manure spreaders, wagons, and sleds were sometimes just left outdoors, often they were housed, especially those with wooden parts. The equipment sheds of this era often were built with balloon-framed rear and side walls and large sawn posts set on stone or concrete footings to support the open front.

By the early 1920s these sheds were being used to store tractors, mechanized equipment, wagons, trucks, and even automobiles. Many of those built for sheltering implements since the mid-twentieth century are pole barns, supported by preservative-treated utility poles sunk into the ground.

Garages

With the purchase of a Model T or other automobile during the 1910s, many farmers built garages on their farms. Because of the risks of fire from gasoline and other combustible fluids, these are typically separate one-story structures with gable or hipped roofs. Early single garages measure about twelve by sixteen feet, although double garages are very common on farms. Large sliding or hinged doors, typically eight or nine feet wide, open at one end. Overhead doors that run on tracks became popular on garages in the 1950s. Inside, floors are typically of concrete or wood, with a workbench and storage area along one wall and small windows above.

In 1928 it was observed that "for some reason, the garage either on the farm or in town seems to be built without any regard to appearance."[7]

Fig. 5-20. Two-bay garage, circa 1930, Richmond, Vermont.

Fig. 5-21. Hipped-roof, two-bay garage, circa 1920, Charlotte, Vermont.

Fig. 5-22. Fireproof three-bay garage constructed of galvanized steel, circa 1920, Canterbury, New Hampshire.

Shops

Known as the shop, workshop, carpentry shop, toolshed, blacksmith shop, or machine shop, these small, well-lighted buildings provide a heated space for making and repairing furnishings, tools, and equipment, as well as for earning outside income through various trades. Products might include shingles, baskets, barrels, harnesses, wrought iron work, shoes, furniture, and wagons.

Fig. 5-23. Blacksmith shop, circa 1848, Moretown, Vermont.

Fig. 5-24. Blacksmith shop, circa 1880, Waitsfield, Vermont.

Typically one-and-a-half stories with a gabled front, an easily accessible doorway, and windows all around, most shops have a chimney for venting a cast iron wood or coal stove. Although many shops are separate buildings, in Maine and New Hampshire the shop is often located in the wing that connects the house to the barn.

Carpentry shops are usually set off the ground, with ventilation below the wooden floor to prevent dampness inside and an open loft above for drying lumber. Blacksmith shops, however, often have dirt floors and large hinged or sliding doors on one end, which open to allow a horse to be shoed inside. These are nearly always separate buildings, however, due to the ever-present risk of fire.

Farm shops reflect the trend toward diversification into home industries that occurred on many New England farms during the nineteenth century. In 1823, farmers were offered the following advice:

> *It is of very great importance to a farmer to have a shop in which he can work in rainy weather and in the winter season. . . . I am convinced that*

most of our farmers would make more money if they made a point of carrying on some mechanical business in the winter. . . . *New England farmers, as a class of people, are perhaps the most ingenious in the known world; but from fall to the spring little comparatively is to be done in agriculture, and consequently, they do but little. What they get in the summer they too often spend in the winter by contracting a habit of lounging in stores and taverns.* "When people have nothing to do the Devil sets them to work." . . . *Our shoes, hats, clothes, ploughs, carts, sleds, and indeed all our implements of agriculture and most kinds of household furniture should be made in winter.*[8]

An article published in 1842 noted:

In addition to the other buildings, every farmer should have a work-shop, with a carpenter's bench and vise in it, and a tolerable set of tools with which to repair and construct various implements as his ingenuity or wants may suggest. A small forge or bellows may be added, with an anvil, and a few blacksmith tools.[9]

Fig. 5-25. The work-bench is the focus of activity inside the workshop. This 1852 illustration shows the bench with a vise at the left and the basic carpentry tools of the period.[10]

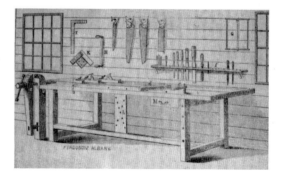

Although a somewhat cluttered workshop was probably the norm on most farms, an 1852 farmer's manual offered the following optimistic verse:

> *The farmer's workshop now our notice claims;*
> *The work-bench, screw, the yawning jaws and planes,*
> *Augers to bore, chisels to mortise, grinning saws*
> *To cut and rip, hammers with potent claws;*
> *The shaving-knife, and set of bits and brace,*
> *All well arranged, each in its proper place.*[11]

Workshops also were incorporated into larger outbuildings, especially on connected farm complexes. As this 1871 description notes, these buildings also served as tool houses:

In this building, all minor tools may be arranged on shelves, or in appropriate niches, where they can at once be found, and will not be exposed to theft.[12]

As the economic viability of agriculture waned and mechanization increased on New England farms during the second half of the nineteenth century and the early twentieth century, the growing importance of the farm workshop is reflected by its frequent mention in the agricultural press. Supporting the development of home-based crafts, trades, and hobbies, the shop became a classroom for passing along mechanical skills to future generations and a laboratory for tinkering and even inventing important mechanical devices.[13] The shop also provided an important refuge outside the house, especially for men and boys, during slack times. As a farmer observed in his diary in 1861:

Fig. 5-26. Carpentry shop, circa 1880, Addison, Vermont.

Fig. 5-27. Combined farm workshop and garage, circa 1920, North Kingstown, Rhode Island.

C. broke the forward bolster of my old wagon yesterday, bringing back wood when he drew F.'s hay home. But a few hours in the farm-shop gave us a new and better one, at but a slight expense, compared with what it would have been without that "institution." Both boys have become pretty good workmen, and C. can even do very handsome jobs of cabinet work.[14]

The *American Agriculturalist* claimed in 1874:

A chest of tools and a tool shop will pay for themselves every year, provided you keep the tools in good order and in their proper places. This is

*an age of machinery, and every farmer should be more or less a
mechanic.*[15]

As technology changed, so did the role of the shop, as was noted in 1928:

*The farm shop is valuable in the busy season for emergency repairs, and
during the winter season for thorough overhauling of all of the farm machinery. In many localities the village blacksmith is gone, and it is becoming difficult to secure quick repairs.*[16]

Piggeries

Also known as the pig house, pig shed, or hogsty, the earliest shelters for pigs
and hogs were often small rough huts or sheds extending from the side of a
barn opening to an enclosed pen. Samuel Deane made these recommendations about the design of the hogsty in 1797:

Fig. 5-28. Often pigs
are provided with only
a small shed in their
sty, Kingston, Rhode
Island.

*The ways of construction of these houses are various: But the best are those
which are framed and boarded. The boards, that the swine not gnaw
them to pieces, should be of some harder wood than white pine, and they
should be fastened with ribbings and spikes. Whatever construction of
sties, they should have always have one part close and warm, with a tight
roof over it; and the other part open, in which a trough is placed. Swine
will not well bear to be wholly secluded from the weather and sunshine;
and it is hurtful to them to have a cold and wet lodging; more hurtful
than many people are ready to imagine.*
    The floor of a sty should be very tight, to prevent the loss of manure; or

else it should be mounted so high above ground, that the manure may be easily pulled out from under it. . . . If planks be thought too expensive for flooring, a good and very durable floor, may be made of flat stones, bedded in clay, that the manure may not soak into the ground. But none of the rocks should be so small, that the largest hog can stir them with his nose. . . . In feeding hogs, their food is often wasted, and so dirtied as to be spoiled, by their standing with their feet in the trough, and by their scuffling with each other. This may be easily prevented. Let the trough be so spiked to the floor, or otherwise made steady, that they cannot displace it; and let a piece of joist be so framed in over the trough, that they cannot stand over it; but can put their heads under the joist into the trough.[17]

Although some farmers used their pigs to mix manures in horse barn cellars, separate structures also were common. Small piggeries were designed much like oversized doghouses, opening directly to a pen equipped with watering pans and feed troughs. Few examples of small nineteenth-century pig houses survive; however, several examples of larger piggeries have been identified.

Larger piggeries were typically divided into pens inside, each with access to a separate outdoor yard through a small, low opening in the wall. Access to the yards could be controlled with vertically sliding doors. These large

Fig. 5-29. T-shaped piggery with a workshop and cooking room in the front, circa 1885, Cavendish, Vermont.

Fig. 5-30. View inside a circa 1885 piggery in Cavendish, Vermont, showing the feed cooking room. Note the feed cooker just to the right of the doorway that leads to the pig pens. This wood-fired cooker had a sheet metal flue pipe connected to the chimney at the upper right. The workbench at the left and the anvil at the lower right reflect the use of this space as a farm workshop.

piggeries often had a separate room with a chimney for a stove to cook grains and root crops for the swine.

The importance of providing adequate shelter for pigs was often discussed in the agricultural newspapers of the nineteenth century. As L. F. Allen observed in the *American Agriculturalist* in 1842:

> *the piggery or hog pen, if not a large establishment should not be at a great distance [from the dwelling]. . . . In its rear ought to be a comfortable yard for the hogs to range at proper seasons. . . . I would suggest the general plan of a main entrance at the gable end by a hall running through its entire length, with the stalls or pens on each side, and the swill or feeding troughs next to the passage. The building should be at least twenty feet in width to admit stalls on each side of the passage, or hall, and any length required for the number of swines to be fattened. Over head, corn or other grain, or various farm products may be stored.*[18]

The *Maine Farmer* offered this description of a model piggery in 1858:

> *The piggery has convenient pens, and with yards in the rear; the feeding room has a boiler for cooking food, boiling water, &c., and is to be ventilated by the windows on each side.*[19]

Fig. 5-31. Piggery, showing low doors leading from the pens to the yards, circa 1885, Cavendish, Vermont.

In 1868 farmers were advised that:

> *No farmery is complete without a well-arranged piggery, which consists of a grain-room, a root cellar, a cooking-room, a feed-room, a sleeping-room—all under cover.*[20]

Slaughterhouses

Although the slaughtering of livestock was often conducted outdoors, small slaughterhouses were built on a few New England farms. Some were simple gable-roof buildings located far enough away from the farmhouse to avoid complaints about objectionable odors and flies. Slaughterhouses were also attached to other farm buildings, for convenience.

Fig. 5-32. Slaughterhouse and shop, circa 1890, Rokeby Museum, Ferrisburgh, Vermont.

Fig. 5-33. The large wooden wheel above provides sufficient mechanical advantage for the crank below to hoist a carcass for butchering in this nineteenth-century slaughterhouse at Rokeby Museum in Ferrisburgh, Vermont.

The characteristic identifying feature of a nineteenth-century slaughterhouse is a large wooden hoist wheel for lifting carcasses. These range from four feet to over six feet in diameter. A small rope runs in a groove or in Y-shaped wrought iron guides around the circumference of the large wheel. As this rope is lightly pulled or winched from below, the long shaft of the hoist rotates, winding up a thicker rope connected to the heavy load.

By the late nineteenth century the growth of the western livestock ranching and large commercial packinghouses diminished the use of slaughterhouses in New England. Those built or adapted during the late nineteenth and early twentieth centuries often have concrete floors with drains to capture the offal and the blood.

Smokehouses and Ash Houses

Typically, a small windowless masonry building with small elevated door and a gable roof, smokehouses were used to smoke hams, turkeys, beef, and other meats. Inside, at the lower level, is an ash pit where ashes were collected for potash to make soap and gunpowder.

The smoldering fire was either made in an enclosed area inside or in a firebox that was accessible to the outside through a small iron door. Smokehouses with outside fireboxes often have flues that direct the smoke to where the meat was hung from the rafters on nails or hooks. Because of the risk of fire, most smokehouses stand separately in a convenient location that can be easily watched and tended.

After being soaked in a brine pickling solution for about two months, hams would be smoked for ten to twenty days. The preferred fuels for gener-

Fig. 5-34. Stone smokehouse and ash house, circa 1820, Ferrisburgh, Vermont.

Fig. 5-35. This diagram of a smokehouse was published in the *American Agriculturalist* in October 1880. The accompanying article notes that the roof ventilator is more ornamental than functional. A low wall divides the floor, with an ash pit toward the rear. A flueless brick and stone fireplace stands inside the front area.

ating smoke included maple, hickory, and corncobs.[21] The *Cultivator* published these descriptions of a smokehouse in 1865:

> *It is built of brick with a stone basement for ash-pit from the smoke-house above, and through which ashes may be poured down. For smoking meat, a fire is built on this ashes, where it may be perfectly controlled, and the smoke rises above. A ventilator surmounts the building, which is closed or opened at pleasure, to prevent dampness so common otherwise with brick smokehouses on the one hand; as well as a too free escape of smoke on the other.*[22]

> *Ashes kept in a brick or stone building become damp, which injures them for soap-making. I recommend (from experience) a building of wood, the four corners of which rest on blocks of stone, which raise the building a few inches from the ground. The lower half is lined with brick, and the*

Fig. 5-36. Smokehouse with brick walls, a stone base, and a cast iron door, circa 1850, Plymouth Notch, Vermont.

Fig. 5-37. Stone smokehouse, circa 1875, Salisbury, Vermont.

floor, which is of stout oak, is also covered with brick. This secures it from any fire in the ashes, and it is perfectly free from any dampness. The fire for smoking the meat is made in an old iron pot, which is set down nearly to the floor, as far away as from the meat as may be, and is readily covered, in part, to secure a slow fire. The door is in the upper half of the building, above the lining. The brick lining is laid in mortar made of clay instead of lime and sand, and is not affected by any chemical action of the ashes.[23]

Sheep Barns

English settlers first brought sheep to the region, mainly for the lamb, mutton, and wool used domestically. Following the English tradition, it was generally recognized that sheep needed abundant fresh air and easy access to pastures to stay healthy. As long as the flocks were small, the sheep could be housed in the main barn if necessary, along with other farm animals.

But the New England climate could cause problems. Indeed, Samuel Deane's book on farming, published in Boston in 1797, makes no reference to sheep barns. He does offer the following advice:

Fig. 5-38. Mid-nineteenth-century
sheep barn, Richmond, Vermont.

If any cold rains happen after shearing, the sheep should be put up in a warm house. For if they be left abroad, it is apt to be fatal to them.
  But Mr. Young thinks they are apt to be hurt by being kept too warm that they should never be confined to a house, but always have the door open, that they may be in the house or the yard as they choose.[24]

For larger flocks, farmers tried simple open structures or small hay barns flanked by open sheds. One article on sheep management, published in the *New England Farmer* in 1823, notes:

> *My practice is to keep sheep sheltered from the rain by open sheds, and shut up the sheep and lambs about one week in a warm stable; and when they are a month old, they will eat hay with the flock.*[25]

But the merits of the open design were soon questioned, especially in New England, where the severe winters prompted sheep farmers to construct barns for the sheep and their fodder. As was noted in 1845:

> *The construction of barns, as well as with dwellings, will always vary, depending on the taste and means of the proprietor. Where the climate is severe, and subject to considerable depth of snow, making it difficult at times to travel a distance to the sheep-folds, a large barn capable of sheltering all the sheep, as well as their provender, is certainly desirable, and would be preferred to several, especially if placed remotely from each other. But it is a question, however, whether the extra time consumed in carting the hay to fill one of these mammoth barns will not more than overbalance this inconvenience.*[26]

With the introduction of the Merino breed during the early nineteenth century, sheep farming became a lucrative activity for many New England farmers. Noted for their long, soft fleece, Spanish Merinos had been jealously guarded in Europe until William Jarvis, the American consul in Lisbon, imported several thousand to this country in 1809 and 1810. He established a flock of over three hundred sheep at his farm in Weathersfield, Vermont. These were soon bred and distributed to farms in the region.

The following account by William Jarvis, published in 1837, describes his sheep farm structures:

> *Attached to my barns I have sheds connected with large yards; in those yards I place my racks. . . . I leave the doors of my sheds open, and let the sheep go in and out when they please. My sheds are occasionally strawed to prevent their becoming very filthy, and there is no waste in so doing, as all the best of the straw the sheep will eat before laying upon it.*[27]

With the opening of the Champlain Canal in 1823, connecting Lake Champlain with the Hudson River and New York City, and with the 1824 tariff on woolens, the Champlain Valley of Vermont became one of the country's leading sheep-raising areas. Forests were cleared, and hills and mountains became pastures. By 1836, Vermont had over a million sheep.[28]

As woolen mills were established on New England's rivers, demand for the fleeces continued to grow. The fleeces, shorn from the sheep once a year, were compressed and often stored in a finished wool room in the attic of a farm outbuilding until being sold. With plastered walls and ceilings to deter rodents, the rooms often had a trap door in the floor through which the wool was dropped down into a wagon for shipping.

The Panic of 1837 triggered a dramatic fall in wool prices, and in a few years the boom turned to bust. In 1846 the protective wool tariff was repealed; and the westward expansion to inexpensive land in the American West, together with competition from Australia, brought a rapid decline to the New England sheep production. As an 1848 government report noted:

> The productions of the dairy are increasing in the same ratio that that of wool is decreasing, in consequence of the low prices of the latter and the enhanced prices of the former.[29]

The Civil War brought a brief resurgence in interest in sheep farming as a demand developed for wool to replace scarce cotton for clothing and to meet the military needs for blankets and uniforms. Numerous letters about sheep farming published in the *New England Farmer* and other agricultural newspapers during the early 1860s reflect many farmers' interest in setting up new sheep farming operations. One published response offers a very detailed description of the ideal sheep barn as envisioned in 1862:

> *"Subscriber," from Rumney, N. H., wants a plan of a sheep barn of capacity to accommodate 200 or 300 sheep, standing on level ground.*
> *The barn should be at least 40 feet by 60 feet; a floor or driveway 12 feet wide, running through the centre from end to end, leaving 14 feet on each side for leantos. The floor or driveway to be elevated 2 feet, by framing in to the posts an extra tier of timbers for the floor to rest upon. There are two advantages gained by the elevation: first, the pitching off hay from the cart, and second, by giving a good chance for racks to feed in, off*

Fig. 5-39. The open shed on the ground floor and the hayloft above identify this mid-nineteenth-century sheep barn located on the Justin Morrill Homestead in Strafford, Vermont.

the side of the floor. The racks should run the entire length of the barn. Rack rounds should be set 4 inches apart from centre to centre. A crib should be made at the bottom of the rack, about 14 inches wide, with uprights 15 or 16 inches apart, going into the rack nave. If more racks are wanted, put shorter ones across the leantos which will, at the same time, divide the flock if you choose. There will be a good chance for a cellar under the floor, costing but little to dig it, the floor being elevated. When the barn is well underpinned, then fill up the leantos, to the bottom of the sills, with sand or loam, which will be preferable to a floor, making a good place for composting leaves, straw, &c., with the droppings of the sheep.[30]

Wool prices dropped soon after the Civil War. Although many farmers shifted to dairying, especially as the railroads brought easy distribution of cheese, butter, and then fluid milk to Boston and other metropolitan markets, sheep continued to be raised for breeding stock for several more decades.

By improving the quality of the stock through selective breeding, some sheep breeders became very successful. Vermont was soon internationally known for its Merino sheep stock, with large exports going to Australia, South America, and South Africa. Efforts were made to maintain the reputation of the breed with the formation of the Vermont Merino Sheep Breeders Association in 1876.

The ground level of some late-nineteenth-century sheep barns featured low pens to separate members of the flock. The upper level was a hayloft. The following recommendations for designing a sheep barn were offered in 1874:

Unless sheep are carefully provided for, there is sure to be trouble and loss in the flock. . . . It is during the winter season, that the most care and skill are needed, and but little success can be had without a good sheep barn. Such a barn . . . [is] about 20 feet wide, 16 feet high from basement to the eaves, and as long as is desirable. This is intended to store hay or fodder. The post, sills, and plates are all 8 inches square, the girts and braces are 4 inches square, the beams 2 ˜ 10, are placed 16 inches apart, and are crossbridged with strips, 3 inches wide. The hay is piled inside, so that a passage-way is left over the feed-passage below, in which there are trapdoors. The hay is thrown down through these doors, and falls upon a sloping shelf, which carries it into the feed-racks below. The basement under the barn is 8 feet high and is of stone on three sides; the front is supported by posts, 8 inches square, and 8 feet apart. Between each pair of posts a door is hung upon pins, which fits into grooves in the posts, so that the door may be raised and fastened.[31]

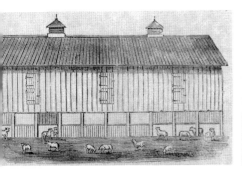

Fig. 5-40. This illustration from the *American Agriculturalist* shows a sheep barn from the 1870s.

Fig. 5-41. As New England sheep farmers shifted to breeding during the second half of the nineteenth century, sheep barns often were built to provide more protection for their prized flock. This sheep barn was built on a stock farm in Cornwall, Vermont, during the 1870s. The wool storage room is in the loft of a nearby carriage barn.

By the end of the nineteenth century and throughout most of the twentieth century, sheep farming continued to dwindle in Vermont and elsewhere in New England. As a result, very few intact nineteenth-century sheep barns survive. Most of those that were not demolished or did not collapse from neglect were converted into dairy barns. There is a chance that the timbers and boards of many sheep barns were incorporated into late-nineteenth-century and early-twentieth-century reconfigured ground-level dairy barns.

Henhouses

Also known as the chicken coop, poultry house, or fowl house, the henhouse was not common on farms until the mid-nineteenth century. Early New England farmers generally kept only small flocks and avoided investing in large-scale poultry farming because of concerns for the effects of the cold climate and the high risk of diseases. Samuel Deane cautioned his readers about poultry in 1797:

> *All kinds of tame birds, as hens, geese, ducks, turkeys, &c. . . . may be considered part of a husbandman's flock: But keeping of great numbers of*

dunghill fowls will not turn to his advantage; as it is certain they will never indemnify him for the corn and grain that are requisite for their support. Yet on a farm a few of them may be useful, to pick up what otherwise would be lost, and in this view they seem to be profitable only part of the year. If confined they will not prosper, though they have a yard of some extent; if not confined they will be mischievous to the garden and field.[32]

A farmer wrote in 1857 about his method of housing poultry:

I keep my hens in a room in the south end of the cellar [of the barn], fourteen feet square, with an open shed outside, with the use of the cellar in the mild weather.[33]

Fig. 5-42. Morning chores. Henhouse with piggery in the background, circa 1885, Cavendish, Vermont. Photo circa 1930.

Fig. 5-43. Henhouse with large sliding windows, circa 1885, Cavendish, Vermont.

Poultry farming grew in popularity during the second half of the nineteenth century, and by the early twentieth century most farms had small chicken coops. These lightly built structures often feature a gabled or shed roof and large windows on the south side. Often chicken coops have a small stove and chimney for heat to protect young chicks during cold weather. Small openings near the ground provide the fowl with access to the yard. Inside are nesting boxes for the layers, as described in this 1858 plan of a model chicken coop for a Maine connected farm:

> *Next comes the laying apartment of the henery, which is furnished with tiers of nesting boxes on each side; a door from this leads into the living and roosting room; the south end of which should either be wholly of glass, or contain two large windows, to attract the warmth of the winter sun.*[34]

Fig. 5-44. Henhouse with outside nesting boxes, circa 1920, East Waterford, Maine.

Although many flocks were allowed free range to grub for small insects, by the late nineteenth century most small flocks were confined and protected by wire pens. The *Country Gentleman* recommended this arrangement for a small flock in 1861:

> *A house . . . eight feet wide, thirteen feet long, and eight feet posts, will accommodate from twenty-five to thirty fowls, and that is as many as any family will find profitable to keep, unless they have a wide range. If confined or restricted in their freedom, a yard one fourth of an acre would be large enough, provided a portion should afford grass, and a dense shade of low trees and shrubs, to which the fowls may retire in hot weather, where they will bask in the sand, and spend much of their time in a sociable and agreeable manner.*[35]

Poultry raising also presented serious risks to those who experimented with improved methods during the second half of the nineteenth century, as was reported in 1874:

> There is something alluring about doing things upon a large scale. The desire to possess a thousand fowls has enticed many men to go into poultry farming as a special business, and to indulge in dreams of an easy and comfortable business if not of wealth. Unfortunately in nearly every case which has come to our knowledge, there has been failure, at first disappointment, then disgust and sickness of heart from the hope deferred, rather than from any inherent impossibility of keeping a thousand fowls as easily as a hundred.[36]

In 1881, the *New England Farmer* published a detailed description of a model poultry house in Newington, Connecticut:

> The room for setting hens is . . . furnished with three tiers of nest-boxes, each fifteen inches square. Each nest has a separate space in front, where food, drink and dust-bath are placed. This prevents the confusion as to nest, and at the same time, allows the hen perfect liberty, which is greatly to be desired. In this room most of the early chicks are cooped. A coal stove is placed here, insuring warmth and comfort for both fowls and chicks. The roof being double gives an upper room, the ends of which are used for cooping either chicks or single birds in the cold season, and for fattening fowls; while the remaining portion is very serviceable as a store-room. The ventilators are at the extreme elevation of the roof, and are so constructed that a plentiful supply of fresh air is constantly obtained. Nearly all of the interior of this house is put together by means of grooves, so that parts may be easily detached, and rooms of different sizes constructed.[37]

Advances in poultry farming were noted in 1886:

Fig. 5-45. Henhouse, early twentieth century, Ferrisburgh, Vermont. Below the windows are small sliding doors that open to allow the hens to grub for food in the yard on the south side of the building.

The breeding of new and choice varieties of poultry has grown to be quite an extensive industry in this country during the past few years.[38]

By 1910, further refinements were being made in poultry architecture:

A small henhouse furnishes no space for exercise, and a large room is too cold during winter nights. The best combination is a small, snug, one-windowed room for laying and roosting, having attached a large, cheap, light shed, the latter, according to location, open south or entirely closed, containing several windows.

Scratching sheds with closed front should have a large, wide door which can be thrown open in mild weather, the hens being confined by an inner door of netting.[39]

Colony Houses

To avoid the spread of diseases among large poultry flocks, some farmers built numerous small "colony houses," each with its own pen. Detailed descriptions of these structures were published in 1910:

Fig. 5-46. Movable poultry colony houses, circa 1940, South Tamworth, New Hampshire.

Farmers in the north who raise poultry extensively usually have started with little capital, and have tried to build the cheapest possible house that would afford enough shelter to secure winter eggs in a severe climate. A typical house of this kind is . . . in use on a colony poultry farm in New Hampshire. . . .

The houses, which, by the way, have been copied liberally by the whole neighborhood, are A-shaped, fifteen by sixteen feet, the narrow side to the front. The seven two by four rafters are eleven feet long, and are nailed at the bottom directly onto the sills, which are two by four and raised a foot or so above the ground on stones. The roof is double, sloping east and west, and is covered first with rough hemlock boards, over which are laid two thicknesses of tarred paper, well battened down, and finally a liberal coat of coal tar over all. The ends of the houses are made in different ways, and some are boarded and shingled, others battened only. Still others are treated like the roof. In the south end on the right side is a door swinging outward, which is left open every day unless the weather is very stormy. A slat door inside is found useful to keep the hens from going out in inclement weather. At the left of the door is the only window in the house.[40]

. . . In some towns of southern Rhode Island poultry farming is the main industry. The farmers keep from two hundred to five thousand chickens, with smaller numbers of ducks and geese, and depend upon them for a living. . . . About two hundred and fifty fowls are assigned to the acre. The house . . . [is] of the simplest plan possible, built of rough hemlock boards and having a small window in front, and a very simple arrange-

Fig. 5-47. Movable colony houses, circa 1930, East Waterford, Maine.

Fig. 5-48. Movable colony turkey hutch, with raised floor, Kingston, Rhode Island.

ment inside. The cost cannot be over twenty dollars per house and may be made considerably less. Some of the houses have a double roof, other are single and made of rough, unmatched hemlock lumber. The roof is of plain boards not shingled, and no roofing or batting paper is used except as an experiment. . . . Built in this style there is no need of providing for ventilation, as the air is admitted through numerous cracks between the boards. The fowls are outside almost every day in the year, as there is very little snow. In the summer, fresh salt breezes keep the air cool and the fowls are vigorous and active all year around.[41]

A moveable house having the floor raised some distance above the ground, thus affording underneath a resting place and shelter from the sun, wind and rain, is for many reasons a decided improvement over stationary houses.[42]

Brooder Houses

Some poultry farms have brooder houses built especially for incubating and raising young. These are often located in sunny sites. Inside are heated pens for the chicks. To provide for continuous production, some brooder houses have numerous pens to keep the various age groups segregated.

Late-nineteenth- and early-twentieth-century brooder houses often had heat distributed through a piped hot water heating system, while electric lamp heaters were being adopted during the 1910s.[43]

Fig. 5-49. Small brooder house, circa 1930, Warren, Vermont.

Fig. 5-50. Twelve-unit brooder house with segregated pens, circa 1920, Ryegate, Vermont.

Converted Poultry Barns

During the 1930s and 1940s, poultry farming was adopted by many farmers in Maine and New Hampshire and elsewhere in New England as a replacement for dairy farming. Many large cow barns were converted into chicken barns with the addition of more floors and numerous windows and dormers.

Fig. 5-51. This circa 1880 dairy barn was converted into a poultry barn around 1940 in Sandwich, New Hampshire.

Multistory Poultry Barns

By the 1930s, large two- and three-story poultry barns were being built for raising broilers and capons for meat and pullets for eggs. These often have a shallow-pitched gable or shed roof and many windows on south side, which

Fig. 5-52. Two-story poultry barn, circa 1930, Sandwich, New Hampshire.

Fig. 5-53. Two-story poultry barn with raised grain elevator, circa 1940, Richmond, Rhode Island.

Fig. 5-54. Large three-story poultry barn with metal sheathing, circa 1960, China, Maine.

are often covered with wire mesh. Mineral-surfaced asphalt paper or shingles typically cover the roof and walls.

Housing thousands of birds, these large structures became virtual factories, with automatic, clock-activated feeders and waterers to reduce labor. Many have built-in grain elevators for storing truckloads of bulk grain.

Very large metal-sheathed buildings became popular for raising poultry by the 1950s. Some are over four hundred feet long and have self-closing vents with fans instead of windows.

6. Farm Buildings for Specialty Crops

Fig. 6-1. Sugar house, circa 1850, Hinesburg, Vermont.

Maple Sugar Houses

As days grow longer during the last weeks of winter and the warmth of the sun thaws the crusty snow, sap begins to rise in sugar maple trees, marking the beginning of the sugaring season. The trees are tapped, and the sap, collected in buckets or by modern plastic tubing, is boiled for many hours to make maple syrup or sugar. About forty gallons of maple sap are required for each gallon of syrup.

Before the mid-1800s most maple syrup was boiled in large iron caldrons outdoors near the maple grove, or "sugar bush." Between the 1850s and 1870s, however, the maple sugar house became a common sight on farms in the maple-forested areas of New England, especially as sugarers adopted large metal evaporator pans. These pans are supported over the fire by an "arch," typically constructed of hard bricks and mortar on a stone base. Iron fire doors are usually fitted at the end of the arch nearest the woodshed. The *American Agriculturalist* noted in 1870:

> *These broad, shallow pans evaporate the sap fully twice as fast as the old kettles used to, even when they were set in an arch. Kettles belong to the days of wooden plows.*[1]

Sugar houses provided many advantages over outdoor boiling. As one Hardwick, Massachusetts, farmer observed in 1870:

Fig. 6-2. This interior view of a sugar house, published in the *American Agriculturalist* in 1870, shows a metal evaporator pan supported by a brick arch with a brick chimney beyond. A trough for storing fresh sap stands to the left. From *American Agriculturalist,* February 1870, 59; courtesy of Bailey-Howe Library, University of Vermont.

Fig. 6-3. Interior of circa 1850 sugar house with a twentieth-century evaporator pan and flue pipe, Hinesburg, Vermont.

Fig. 6-4. Sugar house, early twentieth century, Fairfax, Vermont.

Fig. 6-5. With a full supply of cordwood in the shed, this circa 1920 sugar house in South Tamworth, New Hampshire, is ready for another boiling season.

I have made sugar out-doors with only a few stones laid up to set the boilers on, and to make a place for the fire, where the wind would blow dust and ashes into the syrup, and have had my hair and eyebrows scorched by a flame suddenly blown into my face by a gust of wind, and from my own experience would advise all sugar makers to have some kind of sugar house.[2]

Fig. 6-6. Sugar house, circa 1950, West Paris, Maine.

The maple sugar house is typically a single-story, gable-roofed building with a large gable-roofed vent on the roof. There is usually a chimney or large steel flue pipe at one end, a door on the side, and a few small windows. A large evaporator pan over a brick-walled firebox arch fills the dirt-floored interior. Often an open woodshed, which also serves as a storage shed for pails and other equipment, is attached to one gable end.

Although once common, nineteenth-century sugar houses are now fairly rare, as these buildings were frequently lost or damaged by fire. Most date from the twentieth century. The common use of recycled materials in these utilitarian farm structures often makes it difficult to determine their age.

Greenhouses

The Crystal Palace, built at the London Exposition in 1851, showed the world how a thin lattice of iron and wood could support acres of glass. During the second half of the nineteenth century this technology was applied to the construction of greenhouses on farms and estates in New England. By

Fig. 6-7. Span-roofed greenhouse with an iron frame, circa 1910, Abington, Connecticut.

sheltering the plants and extending the growing season with these buildings, gardeners could start plants (like tomatoes) early enough to mature in New England's short growing season. Horticulturists could propagate varieties of vegetables, flowers, grapes, and fruit trees or raise exotic houseplants or flowers. During the early 1900s many greenhouses were also built for commercial nurseries.

Both open-span and single-roof greenhouses were erected in New England. The open-span design, with glass on both slopes of the roof and on at least one gable end, is typically oriented with the ridge running north-south to allow the most light inside.

The single-roofed, or lean-to, greenhouse is typically oriented east-west, with a glazed sloping roof facing the sun. A brick or masonry wall runs along the north side of the enclosed area to serve as a heat sink. Often a shed is

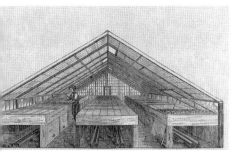

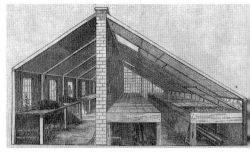

Fig. 6-8. Span-roofed greenhouse designed for propagating grapes, 1867. Note the hinged sash over the plant beds at the right and left. Illustration from Andrew S. Fuller, *The Grape Culturist,* 1867.

Fig. 6-9. Single-roofed greenhouse set up for grape propagation, 1867. Note the brick wall in the center, the workroom at the left, and the hot-water heating pipes below the plant beds. Illustration from Andrew S. Fuller, *The Grape Culturist,* 1867.

used as a workroom and storage area, and the furnace extends along the north side of the greenhouse if the site permits. Single-roofed greenhouses also were built into south-facing hillsides so that the earth would provide shelter during the winter.

Fig. 6-10. Lean-to greenhouse, circa 1920, South Tamworth, New Hampshire.

The typical late-nineteenth- and early-twentieth-century greenhouses, such as those manufactured by the Lord & Burnham Company of Irvington-on-Hudson, New York, a major producer in the Northeast, have a superstructure of cast iron sills and wrought steel rafters that rests on a brick or poured concrete foundation. Angle iron purlins connect the rafters. Between

Fig. 6-11. Greenhouse, circa 1890, Cavendish, Vermont. Although the glass is gone, the remnants of the wooden frame of the open-span greenhouse at the right are supported by a poured concrete foundation. The hip-roofed shed in the foreground houses the furnace and provides storage for clay pots and gardening tools.

Fig. 6-12. This wood-framed greenhouse, erected around 1893 in Charlotte, Vermont, is one of the oldest commercial greenhouses in the state.

the rafters are vertical wooden roof bars, typically made of cypress, that support the panes of glass. These panes are bedded in putty and fastened to the roof bars with glazing nails. The horizontal joints of the glass are simply lapped by about a quarter inch. Sections of roof may open mechanically for ventilation.[3]

Inside, the dirt or gravel floor is often sunken slightly below grade, and the earth is raised slightly around the foundation walls. Iron hot-water heating pipes warm the planting beds, which are constructed of wood or cast iron. Tables for potted plants are typically made of wood or cast iron and slate. A small shed is often attached to one end to house a wood or coal boiler, a workbench for mixing and sterilizing soil and potting plants, and a storeroom for equipment and clay pots.

Hop Houses

Hops have been commercially grown in New England since the seventeenth century to provide flavor for beer. During much of the eighteenth and early nineteenth centuries, Massachusetts led the nation in hop production, and by the 1820s, hop growing had spread to Maine, New Hampshire, and Vermont. Production peaked in the 1870s; then, as soils were drained of their nutrients, the centers of production moved west to New York and then to the Pacific Northwest.[4]

Fig. 6-13. Hop house, circa 1880, Bryant Pond, Maine.

Hop houses, which were built for drying and pressing the cones of the vine, are now very rare in New England. Early hop kilns were typically built of stone and located on a sloping site. Those that survive from the mid-nineteenth century are typically small, gable-roofed wooden buildings. Some are one-and-a-half-story buildings on a level site, while others stand on a sloping site to provide easy access to two stories. Inside is a slatted floor where the hops could be spread out for drying by a cast-iron stove. In one-and-a-half-story hop houses, the hops were dried in the loft; the two-story examples typically have the stove in the lower level.[5]

A detailed description of hop drying was published in the *New England Farmer* in 1823:

A kiln for the purpose of drying hops should be at the side of a hill or rising ground, so that the top should be about nine feet from the bottom, twelve feet square at the top, tapering on all sides to about three and a half feet at the bottom in the clear, *built up tapering, with stone laid in lime mortar, and plastered with clay from top to bottom with an aperture at the bottom about the size of the mouth of a common oven, for the convenience of putting in the coal, firing it, and regulating it afterwards.*

Upon the stones at the top, is placed a sill of four pieces of timber of about eight inches square, and of course about twelve feet long, that being the size of the kiln at the top, upon which you place strips of boards, half

Fig. 6-14. Hop house, circa 1850, Charlestown, Vermont.

Fig. 6-15. Hop house interior, showing slatted ceiling for drying hops in the loft above, circa 1850, Charlestown, Vermont.

inch thick and two inches wide, and within three an a half to four inches of each other, over which you stretch tow or coarse linen cloth, for a bed to place the hops upon, for the purpose of drying, and under which, at the bottom of the kiln, is made a charcoal fire, regulated at the discretion of the man who attends the drying. It will of course be necessary to have a board round the kiln at the top, of about one foot high, to confine the hops on the bed. I think it would be a further improvement to have a covered roof, and open at the sides, to protect the hops in case of rain, while they are drying.[6]

Potato Houses

Until the late nineteenth century, potatoes were typically stored on the farm in the cool, dark basements of houses or barns or in root cellars or pits. Much of the crop was converted to starch in starch mills as early as the 1840s. Large-scale commercial potato production for food grew rapidly during the late nineteenth century as the nation's urban population swelled. To meet the demands of the market, farmers built separate potato houses to store part of their crop from the fall harvest until they shipped the potatoes.

Although potatoes were grown throughout New England during the eighteenth and nineteenth centuries, by around 1900, Aroostook County, the northernmost part of Maine, became one of the nation's leading potato-producing areas. Potatoes thrived in the cool, damp climate and light limestone soils. In 1909, Maine produced nearly 30 million bushels. This was

Fig. 6-16. Aroostook County potato house with eaves-side entry, circa 1910, New Canada Plantation, Maine.

Fig. 6-17. Shingled potato house, circa 1900, Bridgewater, Maine.

Fig. 6-18. This L-shaped potato house with asbestos cement siding in St. Agatha, Maine, probably dates from circa 1920.

Fig. 6-19. Potato house interior, showing wooden bins, circa 1910, New Canada Plantation, Maine.

almost twice as much as the combined production of the rest of New England. Large-scale potato farming also continued in Rhode Island and Connecticut through the twentieth century.

In addition to the farm barn, granary, and equipment shed, nearly every potato farm had a potato storage house. Buried in a hillside or knoll, with soil mounded around the stone or poured concrete walls to keep the interior from freezing during the late fall and winter, the typical Maine potato house

Fig. 6-20. Circa 1920 potato house interior with wooden potato storage barrels, St. Agatha, Maine.

Fig. 6-21. Concrete block potato house, circa 1920. New Canada Plantation, Maine.

Fig. 6-22. Potato house, circa 1920, South Windsor, Connecticut.

Fig. 6-23. The upper level of this circa 1940 potato house in Duxbury, Vermont, was used for equipment storage and maintenance.

Fig. 6-24. Potato house and farm shop built entirely above ground, circa 1940, West Kingston, Rhode Island.

Fig. 6-25. Concrete potato house, circa 1960. Windsorville, Connecticut.

had a gambrel roof extending low to the ground. Often wooden or metal ventilators were mounted on the roof.

Large doors on the lower gable end open to a work area where the potatoes were sorted and packed into barrels. The potatoes were stored in wooden bins that were filled through trap doors in the floor of the upper level. Farm implements could be stored in the upper story. A small cast iron stove connected to a chimney was often used for heating the interior so that the crop would not freeze during the winter. Some Maine potato houses are T-shaped, with extended entrances at the lower level.

Fig. 6-26. Steel potato house, circa 1970, St. Agatha, Maine.

Similar buildings were built by potato farmers elsewhere in New England. Examples from the 1920s and 1930s often have walls of concrete block. Wood-framed and metal potato houses constructed entirely aboveground became popular during the second half of the twentieth century, especially for farms on flat terrain.

Tobacco Barns

Indigenous to North America and grown by Native Americans, tobacco was cultivated by European colonists in New England in the seventeenth century. By the 1830s, tobacco production for cigars became an important crop

Fig. 6-27. Air-cure tobacco barn, circa 1870, Whately, Massachusetts.

in the Connecticut River Valley. The market went through many boom and bust cycles during the nineteenth and early twentieth centuries as smokers' tastes for cigars changed and weather and plant diseases affected the size and quality of the crops.

The Connecticut River Valley saw a dramatic growth in tobacco farming immediately after the Civil War, but as more and more farmers switched to growing tobacco, a glut soon developed, leading to a dramatic fall in prices. As the *American Agriculturalist* reported in 1874:

> *The magnificent castles in the air which have been erected during the past few years by the over-sanguine tobacco growers now lie in ruins. The unfortunate builders are disappointed and disgusted. It was ever thus with growers of specialty crops. For a few years large profits tempt greater ventures and then come excessive crops for one or two seasons and the prices go out of sight. . . . When the surplus is worked off it will doubtless be again profitable. Tobacco is a risky crop.*[7]

Another commentator in the same year remarked on both the decline and the damaging effects of tobacco growing:

> *In a recent trip up the Valley of the Connecticut, from its mouth to St. Johnsbury, we noticed the diminished size of the tobacco fields in Connecticut and Massachusetts. This is attributed to the low price of the weed, the lateness of the season, and the difficulty getting the plants to set. . . . Tobacco in former years paid so largely that the area devoted to it on each farm has gradually increased, and new competitors have each year crowded into the business. We saw evidences of the extent of the business in the new and large tobacco drying shed and drying barns. The acres that ought to be growing fruit and vegetables for human sustenance, are grazing the tobacco worm, and farmers are laboring to check its depredations.*[8]

Fig. 6-28. Late-nineteenth-century tobacco barns with slate roofs stand in a field of broadleaf tobacco in South Windsor, Connecticut.

Built for drying and curing the tobacco leaves used in making cigar binders and wrappers, tobacco barns are found primarily in the Connecticut River Valley of Connecticut and Massachusetts. These long, gable-roofed barns typically have large hinged doors at both gable ends. The side walls have no windows, but to control the rate of curing, boards on the sides can be opened for ventilation. Some tobacco barns also have roof-mounted ventilators. Inside, the barns are lined with racks for hanging bundles of leaves. To maintain the proper temperatures during the curing process, heat may be produced by charcoal fires built on the dirt floor; now propane gas is commonly used.

Fig. 6-29. Propane gas is used to control the temperature for air-curing tobacco inside this late-nineteenth-century tobacco barn in Whately, Massachusetts.

The design of the barns built for air-curing tobacco in the Connecticut River Valley has changed little since the second half of the nineteenth century. This detailed description of their construction was published in 1874:

The barn is of a substantial frame, main timbers 8 x 8 inches—light frames are not strong enough to resist the pressure when filled with heavy tobacco right from the field. . . . [T]he beams are set in the side posts one foot below the top of the plates; below these beams are two tiers of girts, which may be 5 x 6 inches—dividing the whole into three spaces, for the tobacco to hang. These girts extend around and across the building from post to post. On each tier of girts and the beams rest 3 x 5 scantling, running lengthways the building, 4 feet from centres apart, for the lath to rest their ends upon, which holds the tobacco. The roof is boarded and shingled; the siding is good planed pine; one-half the boards (every other one)

Fig. 6-30. Tobacco barn interior, circa 1950, East Windsor, Connecticut.

Fig. 6-31. Tobacco barn with top-hinged wall vents, circa 1950, East Windsor, Connecticut.

Fig. 6-32. Held in position by long hooks, every third board on the wall of this circa 1900 tobacco barn in East Windsor, Connecticut, is hinged on the side to open for ventilation.

Fig. 6-33. Built on a raised, brick-walled foundation, the lower level of this small late-nineteenth-century tobacco barn in East Windsor, Connecticut, serves as a tobacco cellar in which the dampness keeps the leaves soft for easy stripping. This tobacco cellar is lit by the numerous double-hung windows in the foundation walls.

Fig. 6-34. Tobacco storage and sorting barn with tobacco cellar, built in the late nineteenth century, East Windsor, Connecticut.

Fig. 6-35. The stripping shed is marked by its low roof, brick chimney, and location on the north side of this late-nineteenth-century tobacco barn in East Windsor, Connecticut.

tightly nailed, the rest hung with strap-hinges, to afford ventilation or close tight, as necessary; these doors are fastened open or shut with suitable hooks and staples.[9]

In addition to drying the crop, tobacco farmers also constructed barns for storing and sorting the leaves. These barns are built on raised foundations with partially sunken "tobacco cellars" lit by numerous low windows. The dampness of the earth in this dirt-floored area would soften the tobacco leaves, making it easier to strip them from the stalks. Extending from the north end of the tobacco cellar is typically a workroom known as a stripping shed, where workers would strip the leaves from the stalks after curing and then grade and sort each leaf. This 1874 account described its construction and use:

In the growth of the business of producing tobacco, our farmers have found that buildings designed especially for curing the crop, &c. were a

necessity, both for the proper curing and also for stripping, packing and
storing the crop, &c. . . . [T]hey are built of varying dimensions; ours rep-
resents one 32 by 75 feet, holding three full tiers and two part tiers in the
roof, capable of housing about three acres of average growth tobacco. In
one corner is a stripping room 16 ˘ 30 feet, one-half the height below sur-
face of the ground and one-half above, for windows, &c. A chimney rises
from this through the roof, enabling us to put a stove in this room, in
which we may have a fire to strip by in cold weather.[10]

With the decline in popularity of cigar smoking since the 1960s, the demand for New England's tobacco crop has diminished, leaving many tobacco barns abandoned, demolished, or lost from neglect.

Cranberry Screenhouses and Outbuildings

Wild cranberries were an important part of the diet of the Native Americans
living in southeastern Massachusetts. Soon after the arrival of Europeans in
the 1600s, cranberries were being harvested by the English. The first known
efforts to grow cranberries commercially in southeastern Massachusetts occurred during the early 1800s. By the 1830s, cranberry bogs were being
flooded to control diseases and to avoid frost damage; by the 1850s and
1860s, cranberries had become a very popular and profitable crop.[11]

After being picked by hand (the common harvesting method until the
1940s), cranberries were sorted by being "screened" along long wooden
troughs. The mechanical cranberry separator was developed in the 1880s,
and "screenhouses" were built next to the bogs to provide shelter for the

Fig. 6-36. Cranberry
bog with screenhouse,
circa 1900, Carver,
Massachusetts.

Fig. 6-37. Cranberry bounce separator, circa 1885, Carver, Massachusetts.

Fig. 6-38. Cranberry screenhouse, 1912, Carver, Massachusetts.

Fig. 6-39. Cranberry bog pump house, circa 1920, Carver, Massachusetts.

mostly women workers who screened the crop. The cleaned cranberries were put into barrels or wooden boxes and shipped by a teamster to the railhead.[12]

The late-nineteenth-century screenhouses are typically two-story, gable-roofed buildings with wood-shingled walls and double-hung windows with six-over-six panes. There is often a large loading door on one gable end or on the side and several pass doors. Since the cranberries are screened in late autumn, screenhouses usually have brick stove chimneys.

Cranberry bogs are flooded after harvesting to float away dead leaves and damaged fruit. During the winter, flooding protects the plants from being damaged by very cold winds, and brief overnight submersion can offset the effects of hot summer weather. Before the early 1900s the bogs were generally designed to allow water to flood from one to another by opening flume gates in the dikes.

Fig. 6-40. Cranberry bog pump house, circa 1920, Carver, Massachusetts.

Fig. 6-41. Cranberry bog workers' shanty, circa 1903, Carver, Massachusetts.

By the early twentieth century, water levels were controlled by pumps driven by gasoline engines or electric motors. Small, windowless, gable-roofed buildings were constructed to house these pumps. They are located next to the cranberry bogs, often adjacent to a low dike.

In the early twentieth century, cranberry growers often provided housing for their seasonal workers, many of whom came from the Cape Verde Islands. Some shanties were built to house the construction workers who built the bogs. These simple shelters were similar to the primitive tourist cabins of the era, with asphalt shingles on the roof and walls, small windows, and a pass door. The shanties were sparsely furnished with a sink for washing and a kerosene or coal stove for cooking and heating.

Blueberry Farm Buildings

Low-bush wild blueberries are an indigenous plant found throughout most of New England; however, the most important area of commercial blue-

Fig. 6-42. Blueberry fields with farmhouse and barn, circa 1860, Jonesport, Maine.

Fig. 6-43. Blueberry barrens with outhouse for harvesters, Jonesboro, Maine.

berry harvesting is the Down East region of coastal Maine. With its extensive natural blueberry barrens, Washington County, Maine, became a major producer of canned blueberries during the Civil War. After being hand-picked, the blueberries were delivered to canneries or packinghouses in Cherryfield, Jonesboro Station, Harrington, and Machias, Maine.[13]

During the second half of the nineteenth century, canned blueberry production increased and spread to other areas of Maine, the rest of New England, and Canada. Introduced after World War I, frozen blueberries have displaced canned blueberries as the major commercial product.

Since the 1940s, agricultural researchers have worked with growers to develop improved techniques for controlling pests, fertilization, and plant breeding. Today most of New England's wild blueberry harvest comes from managed farms. About half of the total North American wild blueberry crop is harvested in Maine.

Blueberry farming requires few specialized agricultural buildings. The farmhouses and barns associated with this enterprise are typical of those found on most farms of the region. Before the development of mechanical rakes, the harvesting work was done by hand, using scoop-shaped blueberry rakes. As many as fifty seasonal workers would be employed by a grower to harvest the crop during August. These workers were sometimes housed in small camps located near the barrens. Occasionally, outhouses also would be provided for the harvesters on blueberry farms.

After being winnowed in the field to remove stems and leaves, the boxes of blueberries were transported to the packinghouse by horse and cart or more recently by truck. Today the winnowing is done at the processing factory.[14]

Fig. 6-44. Camp for blueberry harvesters, circa 1920, Jonesport, Maine.

Fig. 6-45. Blueberry packinghouse, Jonesboro Station, Maine.

Typically located near a railroad line, blueberry packinghouses are an important associated building type. After being washed and picked over by hand to remove unripe fruit and debris, the blueberries were cooked in large cast iron caldrons and packed into cans. With the shift from canning to freezing that occurred early in the twentieth century, few historic blueberry packinghouses remain.

Apple Farm Buildings

Although many apple barns were older farm buildings adapted for storing and handling the fruit, some were built specially for this purpose. The earliest surviving examples of apple storage buildings in New England probably date to the late nineteenth and early twentieth centuries.

Early apple barns had windows and ventilators that could be opened during the night to bring in cool air, and were closed during the day. Keeping the apples cool in the fall retards the ripening process. The fruit may then be marketed later in the season when its value is increased. Apples were typically stored in barrels or boxes, and stoves were used to heat the barns in the winter to prevent the apples from freezing.

Fig. 6-46. Apple storage barns (*left*), circa 1940, connected to a converted mid-nineteenth-century barn, Panton, Vermont.

Fig. 6-47. Apple orchard retail stand and cold storage building, circa 1860–1970, Foster, Rhode Island.

Ice was used for cooling, especially in the cold storage buildings constructed during the late nineteenth century. To avoid creating a very damp atmosphere inside, the ice was typically stored in a chamber on the second floor. Like icehouses, these apple storage barns were often fitted with a low ventilator on the roof and sawdust- or charcoal-filled walls around the cold storage room. The main part of the apple storage barn typically has no windows; however, a packing- and work-room with windows is often attached.[15]

By the 1940s, large orchards and cooperatives of local growers were building insulated storage structures with electrical refrigeration, windowless concrete walls, and large loading docks for trucks. Many apple orchards also have offices for the wholesale business, as well as small retail stands or stores that offer the crop directly to buyers in the fall.

Many farms with apple orchards also produced cider. The equipment was typically set up in the barn or housed in a small shed. With power supplied by a horse treadmill or an electric motor, the apples were ground into a pomace. After standing exposed to the air in a vat for about a day, to en-

Fig. 6-48. Cooperatively owned apple storage facility, Shoreham, Vermont.

hance the flavor, the pomace was laid onto the cider press in layers separated by straw or coarse burlap and lath. The juice was then squeezed from the built-up "cheese" with a screw press. The cider was allowed to ferment and was stored in barrels in a cool cellar until being consumed or bottled.[16]

NOTES

Chapter 1. Discovering the History of Farm Buildings

1. J. Frederick Kelley, *Early Domestic Architecture of Connecticut* (1924; reprint, New York: Dover Publications, 1963), 3.

2. Abbott Lowell Cummings, *The Framed Houses of Massachusetts Bay* (Cambridge, Mass.: Harvard University Press, 1979), 40–47.

3. S. L. White, "Improvement in Barns," *New England Farmer,* December 1855, 541.

4. A. J. Downing, *The Architecture of Country Houses* (1850; reprint, New York: Dover Publications, 1969), 216, 213.

5. J. H. Hammond, *Farmer's and Mechanic's Practical Architect and Guide in Rural Economy* (Boston: John P. Jewett and Co., 1858), 129.

6. Samuel Deane, *The Newengland Farmer or Georgical Dictionary,* 2d. ed. (Worcester, Mass.: Isaiah Thomas, 1797), 21.

7. Studies of roof-framing techniques in England have demonstrated that the concept of diffusion may describe the distribution of similar cultural traits over an area, rather than being a product of independent local innovation. See J. T. Smith, "The Concept of Diffusion in Its Application to Vernacular Building," in *Studies in Folk Life* (London: Routledge and Kegan Paul, 1969), 60–78. When faced with the diffusion versus antidiffusion (innovation) theories, Smith draws on the roof-framing example. He notes, "In south-eastern England trussed-roofs, i.e. roofs formed by pairs of rafters without ridge-piece or purlins, are universal in big buildings and small from the thirteenth century to the eighteenth century" (65–66). He finds the similarity between these English roofs and those found in the Loire Valley of France so strong that he postulates that the trussed roof design was brought across the English Channel after the Norman Conquest of 1066. Smith has also traced the purlin-roofed, cruck truss construction technique back to pre-Saxon English origins. With cruck construction, the post and rafter are combined in one piece of curved timber.

Another English researcher of vernacular building techniques, Reginald T. Mason (*Framed Buildings of England* [Horsham: Coach Publishing House, 1968], 15–23), states that "regional acceptance of [particular craft] techniques and the rejection of others can hardly be explained . . . through innovation and regional insularity.

The answer may lie in the way in which craft skills are transmitted or handed on. They resemble language to the extent they are taught by demonstration and learned by imitation so that the idiosyncrasies of the teacher are passed on to pupils, thereby consolidated in a generation or two and perpetuated in the long term." Mason then notes the regional distributions of cruck framing and box framing and cites a map drawn by R. A. Cordingley that shows that box frames predominated in the southeastern region of England (roughly including the counties of Sussex, Kent, Essex, Suffolk, Norfolk, and the London area), while cruck frames were common to the North and the West. On p. 51, Mason observes, "The obvious relationship of side purlins to the cruck tradition makes it feasible that they themselves derive from some practice indigenous in pre-conquest times."

8. Studies in the linguistic geography of New England show, for example, that native eastern speakers have tended to drop the *r* sound when pronouncing the word *barn*. See Hans Kurath, *Handbook of the Linguistic Geography of New England* (Providence, R.I.: Brown University, 1939).

9. Edward Shaw, *Civil Architecture* (Boston: Lincoln & Edmands, 1831), 125.

10. Jan Lewandowski, "Industrial, Pre-Industrial Framing," *Timber Framing: Journal of the Timber Framers Guild,* June 1991, 6–7.

11. Shaw, *Civil Architecture,* 126.

12. William A. Foster and Deane Carter, *Farm Buildings,* 2d ed. (New York: John Wiley & Sons, 1928), 96.

13. Solon Robinson, ed., *Facts for Farmers* (New York: A. J. Johnson, 1868), 325.

14. H. R. Bradley Smith, *Chronological Development of Nails: Supplement to Blacksmiths' and Farriers' Tools at Shelburne Museum* (Shelburne, Vt.: Shelburne Museum, 1966), 205–11.

15. Robert Grimshaw, *Grimshaw on Saws* (1880; reprint, Morristown, N.J.: Astrigal Press, 1991), 53.

16. "Plan of a Sheep Barn and Feeding Racks," *New England Farmer,* October 1862, 482.

17. Grimshaw, *Grimshaw on Saws,* 83–92.

18. White, "Improvement in Barns," 540.

19. "The Proper Construction of Barns," *New England Farmer,* 3 March 1841, 273.

20. William D. Brown, "An Hour in a Great Barn," *New England Farmer,* January 1855, 46.

21. "Hints on Building Barns—No. 3," *New England Farmer,* April 1863, 115–16.

22. "Warm Barn," *Maine Farmer,* 21 October 1858, 1.

23. "On the Construction of Barns and Stables," *New England Farmer,* 9 October 1824, 18.

24. White, "Improvement in Barns," 540.

25. Ibid.

26. "A Massachusetts Barn," *American Agriculturalist,* May 1846, 120.

27. "On the Construction of Barns, Stables, &c.," *New England Farmer,* 9 October 1824, 1.

28. "The Proper Construction of Barns," 273–74.

29. "A Modern Barn," *New England Farmer,* May 1857, 233.

30. "Arrangement of Barns," *New England Farmer,* April 1870, 160.

31. Deane, *The Newengland Farmer,* 21.

32. "On the Construction of Barns," 1.

33. L. F. Allen, "Farm Buildings," *American Agriculturalist,* April 1842, 116.

34. "The Proper Construction of Barns," 273.

35. Horace Humphrey, "Barn and Cow Stable," *Genessee Farmer* 14 (1853): 98.

36. Brown, "An Hour in a Great Barn," 46.

37. "Much in a Barn," *New England Farmer,* 548.

38. "Hints on Building Barns—No. 3," 115.

39. Robinson, *Facts for Farmers,* 303.

40. "A Model Barn," *New England Farmer,* April 1852, 272.

41. White, "Improvement in Barns," 540.

42. Foster and Carter, *Farm Buildings,* 277.

43. "Farm Buildings," *Maine Farmer,* 24 December 1857, 1.

44. L. F. Scott, "A New Barn Plan," *Cultivator and Country Gentleman* 27 (7 June 1866): 362.

45. Ora O. Crosby, "A Model Barn," *Maine Farmer,* 29 June 1895, 1.

46. Joe Sherman, *The House at Shelburne Farms* (Middlebury, Vt.: Paul S. Eriksson, 1986), 23.

47. "A New England Farm Home," *New England Farmer,* 31 August 1889, 8.

48. "Barn Construction," *Maine Farmer,* 14 February 1895, 1.

49. U.S. Department of Agriculture, Rural Electrification Administration, *Rural Lines USA* (Washington, D.C.: Government Printing Office, 1960).

50. "Mountain-view Farm," *St. Johnsbury Republican,* 1 July 1896, Burke Centennial Edition.

51. Frank C. Lewis, "Cow Barns," *Breeder's Gazette,* October 1930, 8.

58. Clifford B. Hicks, "The Old Red Barn Is Vanishing," *Popular Mechanics,* May 1948, 137.

59. Ibid., 141.

Chapter 2. Barns

1. Samuel Deane, *The Newengland Farmer or Georgical Dictionary,* 2d ed. (Worcester, Mass.: Isaiah Thomas, 1797), 21.

2. Francis M. Thompson, "History of Greenfield, Massachusetts," quoted in Percy W. Bidwell and John I. Falconer, *History of Agriculture in the Northern United States 1620–1860* (New York: Peter Smith, 1941), 122.

3. Deane, *The Newengland Farmer,* 21.

4. "Barns and Barn Floors," *New England Farmer,* 21 June 1823, 365.

5. Deane, *The Newengland Farmer,* 73–74.

6. Victor A. Conrad, "Against the Tide: French Canadian Barn Building Traditions in the St. John Valley of Maine," *American Review of Canadian Studies* 12 (summer 1982): 22–36.

7. "Plan for a Farm Barn," *New England Farmer,* 8 August 1845, 60.

8. "A New-England Barn," *Cultivator and Country Gentleman,* 25 May 1893, 413.

9. "On the Situation and Construction of Barns," *New England Farmer,* 14 June 1823, 1.

10. L. F. Allen, "Farm Buildings," *American Agriculturalist,* April 1842, 121.

11. "About Barns," *New England Farmer,* March 1858, 132.

12. L. F. Scott, "A New Barn Plan," *Cultivator and Country Gentleman* 27, 7 June 1866, 362.

13. *New England Farmer,* 21 October 1858, 1.

14. "A Modern Barn," *New England Farmer,* December 1857, 233.

15. "Improvement in Barns," *New England Farmer,* December 1855, 540.

16. Scott, "A New Barn Plan," 1–2.

17. "About Barns," 132.

18. "Much in a Barn," *New England Farmer,* December 1857, 548.

19. "About Barns," 132.

20. "Model Farm Buildings for a Maine Farmer," *Maine Farmer,* 2 December 1858, 1.

21. "Hints on Building Barns—No. 3," *New England Farmer,* April 1863, 115.

22. Solon Robinson, ed., *Facts for Farmers* (New York: A. J. Johnson, 1868), 303.

23. "Plans of Barns," *Cultivator and Country Gentleman,* 8 June 1871, 355.

24. "Shaker's Barn," *New England Farmer,* 31 August 1830, 54.

25. "A Splendid Barn," *New England Farmer,* January 1855, 50.

26. "New Hampshire Agricultural College Barn," *Maine Farmer,* 7 June 1894, 1.

27. "A Barn to Save Labor," *Maine Farmer,* 16 March 1893, 1.

28. "The Model Barn of Maine," *Maine Farmer,* 16 April 1896, 1.

29. "Farm Buildings: Large Three Story Barn," *Cultivator and Country Gentleman,* 14 February 1867, 114.

30. C. Chamberlain, "Farm Buildings of Calvin Chamberlain, Foxcroft, Including Octagonal Barn," *Maine Farmer,* 15 July 1858, 1.

31. John E. Taylor, "A Round Barn for Economy," *Breeder's Gazette,* April 1914, 768.

32. Conrad, "Against the Tide," 22–36.

33. E. Burnett, "Construction Details of Modern Barn and Dairy Establishments," in *Cyclopedia of American Agriculture,* ed. L. H. Bailey (New York: Macmillan Co., 1907), 256.

34. Fred C. Fenton, "A Handy Barn with Gothic Roof," *Dairy Farmer,* 15 January 1927, 40.

36. Clifford B. Hicks, "The Old Red Barn Is Vanishing," *Popular Mechanics,* May 1948, 137–42.

Chapter 3. Outbuildings

1. "Facts and Observations Relating to Agriculture and Domestic Economy," *New England Farmer,* 7 June 1823, 353.

2. "Farm Buildings," *Maine Farmer,* 2 December 1858, 1.

3. See Thomas C. Hubka, *Big House, Little House, Back House, Barn* (Hanover, N.H.: University Press of New England, 1984).

4. "A New-England Barn," *Cultivator and Country Gentleman,* 25 May 1893, 413.

5. Samuel Deane, *The Newengland Farmer or Georgical Dictionary,* 2d. ed. (Worcester, Mass.: Isaiah Thomas, 1797), 78.

6. "Farm Buildings," 1.

7. "A Butter Dairy," *American Agriculturalist,* March 1874, 96.

8. "Farm of Mr. Lansing Millis at Oak Grove," *New England Farmer,* 17 May 1884, 1.

9. "Granules," *New England Farmer,* 19 March 1887, 2.

10. "Cheap Ice-House," *Cultivator* 13 (December 1864): 380.

11. Solon Robinson, ed., *Facts for Farmers* (New York: A. J. Johnson, 1868), 297.

12. Theda Dingley, "Summit Farms of Maine," *Sun-Up: Maine's Own Magazine,* May 1926, 11.

13. "Agricultural Property Types," in *Vermont Historic Preservation Plan* (Montpelier: Vermont Division for Historic Preservation, 1989), 95–97.

14. "Spring-Houses," *American Agriculturalist,* October 1874, 380.

15. Deane, *Newengland Farmer,* 240.

16. Robinson, ed., *Facts for Farmers,* 321.

17. L. F. Allen, "Farm Buildings," *American Agriculturalist,* April 1842, 117.

Chapter 4. Buildings for Feed Storage

1. This site is documented in Robert Blair St. George, "'Set Thine House in Order': The Domestication of the Yeomanry in Seventeenth-Century New England," in *Common Places* (Athens: University of Georgia Press, 1986), 345–46.

2. Samuel Deane, *The Newengland Farmer or Georgical Dictionary,* 2d. ed. (Worcester, Mass.: Isaiah Thomas, 1797), 134–35.

3. Solon Robinson, ed., *Facts for Farmers* (New York: A. J. Johnson, 1868), 318.

4. Byron Halstead, ed., *Barns, Sheds and Outbuildings* (1881; reprint, Brattleboro, Vt.: Steven Greene Press, 1977), 177.

5. S. Edwards Todd, "Manner of Framing a Corn-house," in *The Young Farmers Manual* (New York: Saxton, 1862), 50.

6. Robinson, *Facts for Farmers,* 318.

7. Halstead, *Barns, Sheds and Outbuildings,* 128–29.

8. "A New England Farm Home," *New England Farmer,* 31 August 1889, 1.

9. "Another Barn Plan," *Maine Farmer,* 14 March 1895, 1.

10. "A Barn to Save Labor," *Maine Farmer,* 16 March 1893, 1.

11. Thomas Shaw, *Soiling Crops and the Silo* (New York: Orange Judd Co., 1906), 272–73.

12. Ibid., 273–74.

13. Ibid., 272–74.

14. *Green Mountain Silos* (Rutland, Vt.: Stoddard Manufacturing Co., 1908).

15. *Green Mountain Silos* (Rutland, Vt.: Stoddard Manufacturing Co., 1901).

16. Allen G. Noble, "Diffusion and Evolution of the Silo," in *Wood, Brick and Stone* (Amherst: University of Massachusetts Press, 1984), 77.

17. William A. Foster and Deane Carter, *Farm Buildings,* 2d ed., (New York: John Wiley & Sons, 1928), 211.

18. Noble, "Diffusion and Evolution," 78–79.

Chapter 5. Other Farm Buildings

1. Samuel Deane, *The Newengland Farmer or Georgical Dictionary,* 2d. ed. (Worcester, Mass.: Isaiah Thomas, 1797), 317.

2. William D. Brown, "An Hour in a Great Barn," *New England Farmer,* January 1855, 46.

3. "Stable and Carriage House," *Maine Farmer,* 3 June 1871, 1.

4. "Farm of Mr. Lansing Millis at Oak Grove," *New England Farmer,* 17 May 1884, 1.

5. William A. Foster and Deane Carter, *Farm Buildings,* 2d ed., (New York: John Wiley & Sons, 1928), 239.

6. "Hints on Building Barns—No. 3," *New England Farmer,* April 1863, 115–16.

7. Foster and Carter, 210.

8. "Of the Work Shop," *New England Farmer,* 4 October 1823, 76.

9. L. F. Allen, "Farm Buildings," *American Agriculturalist,* April 1842, 117.

10. S. Edwards Todd, *The Young Farmer's Manual* (New York: Saxton, 1862), 367.

11. Ibid., 365.

12. R. L. Allen, *New American Farm Book* (New York: Orange Judd, 1871), 338–39.

13. Some claim the electric motor was invented in a farm shop in Forestdale, Vermont, in 1837.

14. "Leaves from My Farm Diary–VI," *Country Gentleman,* 22 September 1861, 219.

15. "Hints about Work," *American Agriculturalist,* March 1874, 82.

16. Foster and Carter, *Farm Buildings,* 211.

17. Deane, *The Newengland Farmer,* 157.

18. Allen, "Farm Buildings," 117.

19. "Model Farm Buildings for a Maine Farmer," 1.

20. Solon Robinson, ed., *Facts for Farmers* (New York: A. J. Johnson, 1868), 321.

21. R. L. Allen, 485.

22. "Smoke-House," *Cultivator* 13 (January 1865): 35.

23. N. Reed, "Smoke-house," *Cultivator* 13 (May 1865): 151.

24. Deane, *The Newengland Farmer,* 297.

25. "On the Management of Sheep," *New England Farmer,* 4 October 1823, 77.

26. Luke A. Morrell, *The American Shepherd* (New York: Harper & Brothers, 1845), 255.

27. William Jarvis, "Communication from William Jarvis, Esq.," in C. Benton and S. F. Barry, *A Statistical View of the Number of Sheep* (Cambridge, Mass.: Folsom, Wells, and Thompson, 1837), 132–33.

28. C. Benton and S. F. Barry, *A Statistical View of the Number of Sheep* (Cambridge, Mass.: Folsom, Wells, and Thompson, 1837), 33.

29. Percy Bidwell and John Falconer, *History of Agriculture in the Northern United States, 1620–1860* (New York: Peter Smith, 1941), 408.

30. "Plan of a Sheep Barn," *New England Farmer,* April 1862, 192.

31. "A Convenient Barn for Sheep," *American Agriculturalist,* August 1874, 297–98.

32. Deane, *The Newengland Farmer,* 274–75.

33. W. H. Yale, "Much in a Barn," *New England Farmer,* December 1857, 548.

34. "Model Farm Buildings for a Maine Farmer," 1.

35. "Model Poultry House," *Country Gentleman,* 4 July 1861, 13.

36. "Poultry Farming," *American Agriculturalist,* June 1874, 216.

37. "Poultry House of F. H. Corbin, Newington, Conn.," *New England Farmer,* 29 January 1881, 1.

38. "The Poultry Yard," in *The American Farm and Stock Manual* (Springfield, Mass.: Phelps Publishing Co., 1886), 190.

39. George Fiske, *Poultry Architecture* (New York: Orange Judd Co., 1910), 21.

41. Ibid., 30–33.

42. Ibid.

43. Ibid., 41.

44. Ibid., 90–99.

Chapter 6. Farm Buildings for Specialty Crops

1. *American Agriculturalist,* February 1870, 59.

2. "Sugar Making," *New England Farmer,* March 1870, 149.

3. *Greenhouses* (New York: Lord & Burham Co., 1910), 91–94.

4. Michael Tomlan, *Tinged with Gold* (Athens: University of Georgia Press, 1992), 11–33.

5. Ibid., 66.

6. Israel Thorndike, "Further Information on the Curing of Hops," *New England Farmer,* 30 August 1823, 38.

7. "Cultivation of Tobacco," *American Agriculturalist,* April 1874, 139.

8. "Tobacco in the Connecticut Valley—Special Crops," *American Agriculturalist,* September 1874, 338–39.

9. W. H. White, "Tobacco Barn," *American Farmer and Rural Register,* March 1874, 103.

10. Ibid., 102.

11. Robert Demanche, "The Early Cultivators," in *Cranberry Harvest,* ed. Joseph D. Thomas (New Bedford, Mass.: Spinner Publications, 1990), 26–31.

12. Joseph D. Thomas, "Community Harvest," in *Cranberry Harvest,* (New Bedford, Mass.: Spinner Publications, 1990), 64–83.

13. "History of the Wild Blueberry Industry" (Machias: Maine Wild Blueberry Company, n.d.).

14. Peter Drisko, interview by author, Columbia Falls, Maine, 20 July 1992.

15. Samuel T. Maynard, *Successful Fruit Culture* (New York: Orange Judd Co., 1909), 68–69.

16. R. L. Allen, *New American Farm Book* (New York: Orange Judd Co., 1871), 221–25.

INDEX

Place names appear under state names.

Acadian barn, 67
adze, 16–17
agricultural journals, 50
air shafts, 45, 87, 88
American Agriculturalist, 50
apple farms, 196–98
ash house, 159–61

balloon frame, 10, 22–23, 99
band saw, 28–30
bank barns, 42-43
    gable-front, 76–83
    high-drive, 83–86
    late-nineteenth-century eaves-front,
      95–96
    monitor-roofed, 87–88
    side-hill English, 70–71
barn raisings, 5, 22
basements, 40–45, 80–82
    manure, 41, 42, 44, 98
beer, 182
bents, 17, 19
blacksmith shop, 152
blueberry farms, 194–96
board-and-batten siding, 9, 31, 33, 80
braces, 10, 13, 15, 21, 164
bracketed cornices, 9
broad ax, 15
broad hatchet, 15, 16
brooder house, 171
bulk tank, 117
buttery. *See* milk room

buzz saw, 49

carpentry shop, 152-55
carriage barn, 95, 143–49
    Gothic Revival style, 9
cellars, 40–45, 40, 80–82
Champlain Canal, 162
cheese house, 111
chicken coop. *See* henhouse
churning room, 112
cider, 197
circular saw, 27–28
clapboards, 31, 32, 74, 117, 127
colony house, 169–71
concrete, 97
    floors, 98-99, 101
    foundation walls, 44, 97, 101
    silo, 136–38
connected barn, 107–9
Connecticut
    Abbington
      greenhouse, 180
    East Windsor
      horse stable, 147
      tobacco barn, 190
        interior, 190
      tobacco stripping shed, 191
    New Milford
      equipment shed, 150
      silo, 137
    Newtown
      corn crib, 129

University Press of New England publishes books under its own imprint and is the publisher for Brandeis University Press, Dartmouth College, Middlebury College Press, University of New Hampshire, Tufts University, Wesleyan University Press, and Salzburg Seminar.

Library of Congress Cataloging-in-Publication Data
Visser, Thomas Durant.
  Field guide to New England barns and farm buildings / Thomas Durant Visser.
    p.   cm.
  Includes bibliographical references (p.   ) and index.
  ISBN 0–87451–770–2 (cloth : alk. paper). — ISBN 0–87451–771–0 (pbk. : alk. paper)
    1. Barns—New England. 2. Vernacular architecture—New England. 3. Historic buildings—New England. I. Title.
NA8230.V57   1997
728'.922'0974—dc20   96–17230